EL ALAMEIN

'Impeccably reliable . . . lucid and unprejudiced.'
The Times Literary Supplement

'Manages to convey with rare effect the confusion of war without in any way sacrificing the pattern of either thought or action.' *Observer*

'The definitive history of Alamein.' *The Spectator*

MICHAEL CARVER

El Alamein

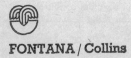

FONTANA / Collins

First published by B. T. Batsford Ltd. 1962
First issued in Fontana Books 1973
Second Impression July 1975

© Michael Carver, 1962

Made and printed in Great Britain by
Wiiliam Collins Sons & Co Ltd Glasgow

TO JOHN HARDING
MY COMMANDER IN THE BATTLE

CONTENTS

ACKNOWLEDGMENTS

I have received help and encouragement from a large number of people, whom I cannot thank individually. I owe a great deal to *The Rommel Papers* and wish to record my thanks to Frau Rommel, Herr Manfred Rommel, General Fritz Bayerlein, Captain B. H. Liddell Hart and Messrs Wm. Collins & Sons Ltd for permission to quote from them, in particular Rommel's letter of November 3rd 1942 to Frau Rommel and Hitler's message of that day. I am equally indebted to Major-General R. W. Knights, Australian Army Headquarters and Mr Gavin Long for providing me with a copy of 9th Australian Division's report on the battle. My thanks are also due to General Westphal for information about the German divisional commanders, and to Colonel di Lauro of the Italian Official History for information about their commanders and organisation. For permission to quote from personal and other accounts I am beholden to Lieutenant-Colonel A. A. Cameron, Mr Peter Luke and *The Cornhill Magazine*, Colonel J. A. Sym and Mr Alistair Borthwick, and to Mr John Montgomery.

M. C.

ILLUSTRATIONS

Winston Churchill visiting Eighth Army Headquarters, August, 1942: with (left) Lieut.-General Alexander and Lieut.-General Montgomery. (*Imperial War Museum*)

Montgomery with Lieut.-General von Thoma, Commander of the German Afrika Korps, after von Thoma's capture, 4 November, 1942. (*Imperial War Museum*)

Field Marshall Erwin Rommel (second from the right) confers with his staff. (*The Associated Press*)

The German army on the battlefield near Tobruk. (*Imperial War Museum*)

Sappers of the Highland Division defusing mines. (*Imperial War Museum*)

Members of the regiment of Gurkhas which fought at El Alamein.

Australian troops attacking under cover of a smokescreen. (*Imperial War Museum*)

A British *Crusader* tank passes a blazing German tank. (*Imperial War Museum*)

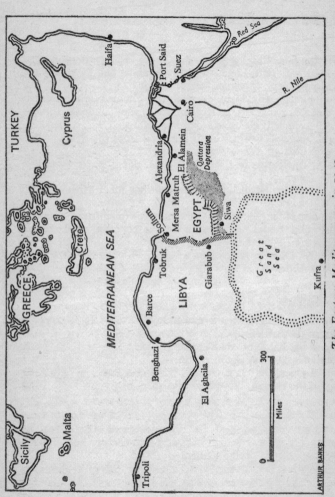

The Eastern Mediterranean in 1942

1 UP AND DOWN THE DESERT

El Alamein is an insignificant station 50 miles from Alexandria on the coastal railway to Mersa Matruh. The station takes its name from the ridge between the railway and the sea, Tel el Alamein, the hill of twin cairns. It was known to soldiers stationed in Egypt before the Second World War as a convenient stopping place for the night on the way to Mersa Matruh. There was no road then, only a track. Opposite the station at El Alamein was one of the few places where it was easy to get down to the beach and refresh oneself with a bathe in the clear blue sea, washing away the dust which covered one from head to foot.

Qaret el Himeimat, 28 miles to the south, was familiar also to the same sort of soldier as an important landmark on the direct 'barrel' track through the desert from Cairo to Mersa Matruh. A barrier, impassable to vehicles except at one or two places, stretched south-westwards from it for 200 miles towards Siwa. This was the Qattara Depression, a vast salt marsh 200 feet below sea level, passable even to camels only in a few places, and flanked on the north, until near Siwa, by a steep and rugged escarpment. From the south-west corner of this salt marsh near Siwa another formidable barrier stretched both west and south for hundreds of miles, the Great Sand Sea.

South and east of these barriers the desert was sand with a smooth crust of gravel. In a lightly loaded truck with desert tyres one could speed over it with ease, except where long sand dunes formed by the wind ran across one's path from north-west to south-east. But the passage of several vehicles cut up the surface until it became a treacherous bog of sand, negotiable only to the skilled, if at all.

North and west of the barrier the desert was quite different. Except close to the sea, where sand dunes and salt marshes prevailed again, it was basically of rock and could support limitless traffic. It was broken up in places by depressions, escarpments and areas of soft sand or tufty scrub, which could limit and confine movement at all times: in the dark without headlights they could make it practically impossible.

The strategic importance of this neck of land between El Alamein and Himeimat, acting as the neck of a funnel through which armies invading Egypt from the west must pass, is obvious to anyone who looks at a map which shows these features. One would have expected it to have been the scene of countless battles down the ages. There is no record of them. The desert, stretching for hundreds of miles to the west, was itself a barrier to invasion before the mechanical age. Even in 1938 experts in Cairo were dogmatic that no more than a brigade could be based in the Western Desert of Egypt for lack of water; but the water was there for those who found where to bore for it and could produce the means to transport it.

How did it happen then that, in the autumn of 1942, the tide of battle between on one side the armies of Hitler's Germany and Mussolini's Italy, and on the other the armies of the British Empire, turned on this 30-mile neck of land? British troops had been stationed in Egypt since 1882, when Sir Garnet Wolseley had landed soldiers from England at Ismailia and from India at Suez and had defeated the Army of the Khedive Ismail at Tel el Kebir while the Royal Navy bombarded Alexandria. Since the Suez Canal had been opened in 1869 Great Britain had paid even more attention than before to the narrow neck of land between the Mediterranean and the Red Sea. When the finances of the Khedive collapsed in chaos and he was forced to repudiate his debts to the foreign bond holders, Britain had invited France to intervene with her to protect the interests of all the European countries concerned. France had refused and Britain had acted alone.

Constantly professing her desire and intention to depart as soon as she had fulfilled her task of putting Egypt's house in order, her troops and her administration remained until a new situation arose in 1914. Egypt was still nominally a dependency of the Sultan of Turkey, when the latter allied herself with Germany in the First World War. Britain, therefore, was forced to declare Egypt's independence from Turkey. The latter's troops, helped by the Germans, at one time reached the Suez Canal itself from Palestine. Throughout the First World War Egypt became the base and centre of great military activity to support the campaigns at Gallipoli, at Salonika, and in Palestine. In the Western Desert a few minor skirmishes took place against the Senussi, roused to action by the Turks and Germans. Here the Duke of Westminster's armoured cars proved the potentialities of a mechanised force in the desert.

After the war and the dissolution of the Ottoman Empire, Great Britain assumed wider responsibilities in the Near East, as it was then called. These, the growing importance of oil supplies, and the advent of the aeroplane, enhanced the importance of Egypt to Britain. Troops remained stationed in Cairo, Alexandria and Ismailia, in spite of agitation for independence.

In 1935 Italy, already installed in Libya, embarked on a campaign of revenge and colonial expansion against Ethiopia. Both Britain and Egypt saw a danger of encirclement by the Fascist powers, and steps were taken to modernise and strengthen the British garrison in Egypt, which at that time was largely an affair of horse and foot.

So it came about that, when Italy joined Germany at the fall of France in May 1940, the British had an armoured division, the 7th, up in the Western Desert, based on Mersa Matruh. Its armoured cars, old Rolls-Royces of the 11th Hussars, not basically different from those the Duke of Westminster had used in the same area some twenty-five years before, crossed the frontier south of Sollum within a few hours of the declaration of war. In support was the nucleus of the Desert Air Force, an army co-operation squadron, a fighter squadron, and three bomber squadrons.

The beginning of the following year saw the utter defeat of the Italian Army in Libya, starting with the Battle of Sidi Barrani in December and culminating at Beda Fomm, south of Benghazi, in February 1941. The Germans suddenly saw the danger that the whole of North Africa might come under the control of the Allies. If the British overran

Tripolitania, they would come into contact with French North Africa, which might well then free itself from the control of the Vichy régime. The situation in the Mediterranean would be transformed.

Hurriedly a small mobile force was assembled for despatch to Tripoli to support the Italians in defending the western province of Libya. Its commander was Erwin Rommel, whose brilliance as the leader of a Panzer division had been shown in France the previous year. This force, originally the 5th Light, later the 21st, Panzer Division was the nucleus of the future 'Deutsches Afrika Korps' (DAK) and of the Panzer Armee Afrika.

The British force in Egypt and Cyrenaica, now including also Australian, New Zealand, Indian and Rhodesian forces, and soon to be joined by South Africans when the campaign in Abyssinia was over, did not proceed to exploit the victory of the Western Desert Force towards Tripoli. Instead its main effort was switched to the vain attempt to save Greece and Crete from German invasion.

While it was preparing to do this, Rommel, against the orders and intentions of both the Italians and the German High Command, struck at the small British force at Mersa Brega at the bend of the Gulf of Sirte. Exhilarated by his immediate success he drove forward, spreading confusion and exploiting it. He forced the withdrawal of the forces in the 'bulge' of Cyrenaica, encircled Tobruk and dashed on as far as the Egyptian frontier at Sollum. Here at last he paused, having recaptured in a few weeks almost all that the Italians had lost in the winter campaign.

He had accomplished military miracles, which were to have a decisive effect on the future of the campaign. First of all he had disregarded the orders of his Italian and German masters and had proved that, if this disobedience led to success, it would be overlooked and even applauded. Secondly, he had overruled all the professional military advice that he was given, particularly from the Staff and the Quartermasters. He had shown that what was not possible by all the rules of reason and calculation could be done by a determined will, speed of action and the exploitation of the confusion caused by a surprise move, swiftly and boldly executed. By then making the greatest possible use of captured resources, he could maintain his force far beyond the distance which the Staff and Higher Command had considered possible. He was to repeat this performance, but it finally led him to defeat.

In May and June of 1941, during and after the disastrous campaign in Greece and Crete, the British had tried and failed to throw Rommel back from the frontier and join up again with the beleaguered garrison in Tobruk. Rommel in turn failed to reduce that fortress. Tobruk itself, and the Royal Navy supplying it, were battered from the air. Not only did it hold out, but the 9th Australian Division which formed the bulk of the garrison was relieved by the British 70th Division and the Polish Carpathian Brigade. The garrison was also reinforced by other British units during the summer.

It was at this time that General Sir Claude Auchinleck relieved General Sir Archibald Wavell as the British Army Commander-in-Chief in the Middle East. One of the new commander's first steps was to order General Sir James Marshall-Cornwall, commanding British troops in Egypt, to press on with the construction of a defensive position at El Alamein. Work on this proceeded slowly throughout the rest of the year. It took the classic form of all defensive positions in the Western Desert, to which Rommel's position on the frontier, which he had just successfully held against two British attacks, was no exception. The principal position, destined for the bulk of an infantry division, lay on the coast, covering the road and protected on its north flank by the sea. The main feature of this position was the observation gained from the ridge of Tel el Alamein over the flat and open ground to the south-west.

The next position, in the centre of the line, was to be fifteen miles to the south-west. It was to include the peak of Qaret el Abd, from which good observation was to be had particularly to the north. The area round it was broken up into escarpments and depressions, which made movement difficult. Between El Alamein and Qaret el Abd the ground

was generally flat. About half-way between the two the
Ruweisat Ridge ran eastwards from just south of a small
depression called Deir el Shein. The ridge was no real ob-
stacle to movement. North of it the ground was flat, with
patches of soft sand and tufty bumps. South of it lay a
plateau-like area of good hard going, the southern edge
of which, later known as Bare Ridge, followed roughly a
line running east for about 12 miles from Qaret el Abd, turning north-east through Alam el Halfa until it finally con-
verged towards the eastern end of the Ruweisat Ridge south
of El Ruweisat station.

The southernmost position was sited to cover the pass
down the escarpment to the Qattara Depression at Naqb abu
Dweis. This was almost twice the height of Qaret el Abd.
Magnificent and awe-inspiring views spread in every direction, but the place itself was inaccessible and troops there
could have little effect on anything but a direct assault
against themselves. Between Qaret el Abd and Naqb abu
Dweis lay steep escarpments and imposing heights. Much
of the area presented great difficulties of movement to a
force travelling west to east. However, once through the
narrow neck of smooth ground just north of Gebel Kalakh,
a flat smooth plain of firm going ran between, on the north,
a series of depressions running south-east from near Qaret
el Abd for nearly 20 miles to Deir el Ragil and, on the
south, a high escarpment as far as Qaret el Himeimat and
then a low ridge running east to Samaket Gaballa. South of
this ridge the ground became softer and sloped down until
it came to the steep edge of the great depression above the
salty, mosquito-ridden oasis of El Maghra.

A mechanised enemy approaching the Alamein line from
the west would find himself naturally funnelled into three
possible avenues; the northern, between the railway and
Ruweisat Ridge; the centre, just north of Qaret el Abd and
then eastwards to the south of Ruweisat Ridge and north
of Alam el Halfa; the southern, north of Gebel Kalakh,
Himeimat and Samaket Gaballa. These avenues would follow
the best going and also generally by-pass the defensive positions, which would have taken about two infantry divisions
to hold.

Such a mobile enemy could not be stopped from passing between and then isolating these 'boxes', as they were sometimes called, which could then be starved or hammered into submission one by one. All their garrisons could do was to shell the enemy they could see with the limited amount of artillery that could be fitted within the perimeter. Any extension of the perimeter, which had to be defended from every direction, greatly increased the number of troops needed to hold it, and particularly the number of anti-tank guns required. The troops within them could not be made mobile without cramming the 'boxes' full of vulnerable trucks. An essential part of the defence was therefore the existence of at least two armoured divisions to operate in the gaps between the defensive positions and to deal with any enemy which might penetrate between them or concentrate against one of them.

Without provision for reserves, therefore, the El Alamein line, as planned in 1941, needed a minimum of two infantry and two armoured divisions.

All this was conceived and the first work begun in the late summer of 1941, while Rommel was preparing to make a final attempt to reduce Tobruk and the British were building up a force round Mersa Matruh with which to resume the offensive. General Auchinleck was under considerable pressure to embark upon this in September and then again in October. However he resisted this pressure in order to be certain that his force, now called the 8th Army and commanded by General Sir Alan Cunningham, was adequately trained and equipped. He chose November 18th as the date to attack. This operation, called 'Crusader', was designed to relieve Tobruk, recapture Cyrenaica, bring much needed air and naval support to Malta and open the way to the clearance of the whole North African coast. It succeeded in all but the last of its aims, but not without difficulty and periods of doubt and confusion.

The situation at the end of it, in January 1942, was an almost exact return to that which had prevailed in February 1941. The German and Italian force, still under the nominal command of the Italians, was back, exhausted and much reduced in numbers, at Mersa Brega. 8th Army, now commanded by Ritchie, had a small force in contact with them there, but held the bulk back in the bulge of Cyrenaica or at Tobruk, where it could more easily be maintained. As in 1941, the force forward of Tobruk included new arrivals, who had relieved the troops exhausted by the operations which had continued almost without pause for close on two months.

Again, as in 1941, the planned strength of the Middle East had had to be diverted to another theatre, this time to the Far East, where Singapore had fallen and Burma was in peril. The effect on the force available for the desert campaign was not as great as had been that of the expedition to Greece a year earlier; but two Australian divisions, the British 70th Division and 7th Armoured Brigade and a number of units had to go, as well as several squadrons of the Royal Air Force.

On January 21st 1942 Rommel repeated almost exactly the operation he had embarked upon with a smaller force the previous year. The results were as immediate and almost as spectacular. However, although successful in driving the 8th Army out of the bulge of Cyrenaica, Rommel did not manage to capture any very large numbers of men or equipment, and this time his advance was checked on a line running south from Ain el Gazala, 40 miles west of Tobruk.

Facing each other on this line, the two sides both began to prepare for a further round. The aim given to Rommel by his superiors was limited to the recapture of Tobruk and to driving the 8th Army and the Desert Air Force back behind the Egyptian frontier, while naturally inflicting as much damage on them as he could.

To the British the principal aim was to re-establish airfields in the bulge of Cyrenaica. The plight of Malta was becoming desperate. Supplies were running low and the loss of the Cyrenaican bulge had made it almost impossible to get ships to Malta from the east. An attempt to get them there from the west had recently cost dear.

For this reason strong pressure was brought to bear on Auchinleck from London to resume the offensive and recapture the bulge as soon as possible. He was most reluctant to do this. He was now convinced that 8th Army would court a third rebuff at Rommel's hands if it attempted such an operation, until it was in a position to exploit success immediately beyond El Agheila. The diversion of a large part of his force to the Far East seriously upset his plans when German successes in Russia were causing him concern over the defence of Iraq's northern frontier. But, after an exchange of views, the War Cabinet accepted the risks involved and it was finally agreed that 8th Army should attack in the middle of May.

As this date approached, however, the outlook became gloomier. Disastrous news came from the Far East: Burma had fallen; there was talk of the Japanese possibly capturing Ceylon; the security of India itself was threatened. Such news seemed to Auchinleck to demand a complete reconstruction of Middle East strategy, and he pointed out the great risks of launching an offensive in Libya at such a time with inadequate armoured forces. But in London the view was taken that the need to relieve Malta was paramount and that Auchinleck was overestimating his difficulties. So on May 10th the War Cabinet issued clear orders to the Commander-in-Chief to launch an offensive in May, as planned, or at the latest early in June, to assist a convoy to Malta in the next 'dark period'.

There can be little doubt that this controversy could have been settled if Auchinleck had been able to go to London as requested. As it was, the good relations between the Prime Minister and the Commander-in-Chief became strained and remained so thereafter.

In the desert the first activity after the position had been stabilised on the Gazala Line had been defensive, originally based on a plan to hold lightly in the forward area and fight the main battle near the frontier at Sollum, abandoning Tobruk. As strength increased and plans for the offensive were made, the original plan was abandoned and a considerable effort made to erect a strong defence, impenetrable to tank attack, at the northern end of the Gazala line. Defensive positions were built and intricate minefields laid covering large areas, to complete which some mines were removed from the old defences of Tobruk itself. The railway from Alexandria and the water pipeline were extended to the eastern perimeter of Tobruk, which became a vast forward base. To cover it the defensive system was extended southwards as far as Bir Hacheim, thus leaving wide gaps between positions in the south which were covered only by minefields.

Rommel watched these preparations and the growing strength of 8th Army with anxiety. He wished above all to avoid a situation in which his opponents could engage the whole of his force and still have sufficient mobile forces to spare to outflank him and cut his supply line to Benghazi and Tripoli. His best chance seemed to lie in forestalling a blow by Ritchie. His intention to do so became apparent in May. With a sigh of relief 8th Army and GHQ put away their plan for an offensive and prepared to receive Rommel on 'ground of their own choosing'. The hazards of launching an attack in the desert were great, and it was therefore with relief and confidence that 8th Army stood ready to receive Rommel.

He moved on the afternoon of May 26th 1942. At first it looked as if he was going straight for the centre as Auchinleck had suggested to Ritchie that he might; but air reconnaissance before last light, and reports from armoured cars and the motor brigade of 7th Armoured Division during the night made it clear that at least a considerable part of his force had turned south towards the Free French Brigade at Bir Hacheim.

In fact the whole of the mobile force of the Afrika Korps had swung south to refuel just before dawn south of Bir Hacheim, intending to drive north-east straight for the very outskirts of Tobruk itself, to Acroma on the west and El Adem on the south. It was a bold plan and half successful, catching Norrie's 30th Armoured Corps unbalanced, its three armoured brigades separated by considerable distances, and 7th Armoured Division, east of Bir Hacheim, still out of its battle positions.

Within a very short time, however, Rommel was in a desperate position. 8th Army was recovering its balance. He had failed to reach his objectives and was hemmed in in a small area east of 8th Army's minefields, almost out of ammunition and with no line of supply. Always a gambler, he now became prudent. Keeping his force concentrated and in hand, he opened a path through the minefields and re-established his line of communication, while beating off the rather ineffective and unco-ordinated attacks delivered against him. Day by day he improved his position, until he had removed the principal thorns in his side, 150th Infantry Brigade of the 50th Northumbrian Division at Dahar el Aslag and the 1st Free French Brigade at Bir Hacheim.

That done, he resumed his original plan and in a series of tank battles reduced 8th Army's tank force to a total of 70 tanks, while he still had over 100 German and about 60 Italian tanks in hand. June 12th was the fatal day, after which it was clear to Ritchie that, with his mobile force destroyed he must move his infantry and the whole administrative machine, built up for the intended offensive, before they all fell into Rommel's hands. It was no easy task.

The desire of all concerned to have their cake and eat it too undoubtedly led to misunderstandings over Tobruk. Auchinleck was determined that Tobruk should not become invested again, but also that it should not be surrendered to the enemy. He gave orders that Rommel was to be held on a line based on the western perimeter of Tobruk and extending south. Ritchie, intending to fulfil the spirit, if not the letter of the order, had already given orders which meant that the fortress of Tobruk would be held and that the forces to prevent it from becoming invested would assemble and re-organise on the frontier, rather than try and do so in the very middle of the mêlée round El Adem. In the event Rommel rapidly cleared an area round Tobruk and delivered a successful lightning attack from the south-east. In so doing he had solved his own logistic problem and immediately set off on a repeat performance of his spoiling attacks from Agheila.

On hearing that Tobruk had fallen, Ritchie decided to base his main defence on Mersa Matruh and to delay only on the frontier at Sollum, to which Auchinleck agreed. Headquarters 10th Corps from Palestine, under General

The Battlefield

ARABS GULF

To Alexandria 28 miles

El Daba
Sidi Abd el Rahman
Tel el Aqqaqir
Rahman track
Kidney Ridge
Tel el Eisa
El Alamein
El Imayid
El Ruweisat
Miteiriya Ridge
Deir el Shein
Ruweisat Ridge
Alam el Halfa
Pt. 102
Barre Ridge
Muhafid
Qaret el Abd
Munassib
Ragil
Samaket Gaballa
Gebel Kalakh
Qaret el Himeimat
Naqb abu Dweis
Qattara Depression

Miles
0 5 10 15

N

ARTHUR BANKS

Holmes, had already been sent up to Matruh to take over its defence. Freyberg's 2nd New Zealand Division was sent up from the Delta and 50th Division and 10th Indian were sent straight back from the frontier to come under his command. All the remaining troops in the area of the frontier were now handed over to 13th Corps under Gott, while Norrie took the headquarters of 30th Corps back first to Matruh and then, when 10th Corps had arrived, to El Alamein to take command of the 1st South African Division and organise the positions there for defence.

Only two days after Tobruk had fallen Rommel crossed the frontier with only 44 tanks. Two days later, June 25th, he was in contact with Gott's 13th Corps south of Matruh. It was on this day that Auchinleck decided to take over command in the field himself, flying up from Cairo and relieving Ritchie of command that evening. Much space had gained 8th Army little time and they were still in a state of confusion, as well as being infinitely weary. In the next two days Rommel dispersed 13th Corps which commanded all the troops outside the perimeter of Matruh, including the New Zealand Division. Within it 10th Corps were surrounded. They broke out and the disorganised formations of both corps swept back to the El Alamein Line. Rommel continued, some of 8th Army travelling parallel, some even behind him. He was finally brought to a halt on July 1st on the defences of El Alamein itself, held by 1st South African Division, and on a position at Deir el Shein, hurriedly constructed and held by 18th Indian Infantry Brigade. Further south the New Zealand Division had collected round the Qaret el Abd position, and 1st Armoured Division, which had taken over command of all the remaining armour, collected itself astride Ruweisat ridge. The Naqb abu Dweis position was held by 9th Indian Brigade, the only brigade under headquarters 5th Indian Division which was near Himeimat. Headquarters 7th Armoured Division was also there but had only 4th South African Armoured Car Regiment under command.

Throughout July fighting continued up and down the El Alamein Line. It was like a boxing bout in reverse. At the start both sides were weak and utterly exhausted. They flailed away but did little damage to each other. As time went on, however, they gathered strength and each thought that he was in a position to deal a knock-out blow. But each time one struck he found the other stronger too, especially in his defence. Mines were laid and positions strengthened. Each successive blow cost more and yet achieved little. Although gaining in strength, the constant battering left them breathless. The round seemed interminable. It was time for the gong, a breather, a drink and a rub-down. 9th Australian Division, which had joined the South Africans in the north, had extended the El Alamein position westwards to include the mound of Tel el Eisa. From here the line ran almost due south through Deir el Shein, east of Qaret el Abd to west of Qaret el Himeimat. The old positions of Qaret el Abd and Naqb abu Dweis were therefore in German hands, as was the narrow neck of good going round Gebel Kalakh. This was the situation at the end of the month when Auchinleck reported to London in these words:

An exhaustive conference on tactical situation held yesterday with corps commanders. Owing to lack of resources and enemy's effective consolidation of his positions we reluctantly concluded that in present circumstances it is not feasible to renew our efforts to break enemy front or turn his southern flank. It is unlikely that an opportunity will arise for resumption of offensive operations before mid-September. This depends on enemy's ability to build up his tank force. Temporarily therefore our policy will be defensive, including thorough preparations and consolidations in whole defensive area. In the meantime we shall seize at once any opportunity of taking the offensive suddenly and surprising the enemy.

2 BRAVE BUT BAFFLED

Long before General Auchinleck's telegram arrived, those responsible in London for the direction of the war had concluded that drastic action was needed to put things right. Since 1940 the Middle East had received everything Britain could spare in men and machines. In every major encounter since the middle of 1941 8th Army and the Desert Air Force had had a numerical and material superiority over the enemy and yet here they were back almost to the Delta of Egypt with the Commander-in-Chief pressing once again for a breather.

The confusion of the battles of the summer, the fall of Tobruk, the capture by the enemy of so many men and so much equipment, the subsequent apparently almost panic retreat to El Alamein, rumours that plans were being made even for the evacuation of Egypt itself, all caused the gravest concern in England as the country entered its fourth year of war.

It was clear too by all accounts, as was only to be expected, that these events had severely affected the morale of the once gay and confident Desert Army. Defeat, withdrawal and the bewildering succession of events since the end of May brought to the surface the tensions, rivalries and suspicions which, in normal times, lie latent in any army. A legend had grown up since then that the Army was hopelessly dispirited and had lost faith entirely in its commanders. This is both an exaggeration and an over-simplification. Few parts of the Army had lost faith in themselves or even in their commanders. Many laid the blame on their equipment: some of this was justified, but a great deal was not, certainly not to the degree that was popularly accepted either then or since.

The most general and the most dangerous tendency was that of different arms or formations to lay the blame on others. In this situation the heterogeneous nature of the Army was

a handicap. The commanders and staffs of all the headquarters above division were, with few exceptions, drawn
from Great Britain, as were all tank units and all units of
the armoured divisions, except for two South African armoured car regiments.

This state of affairs accentuated any tendency there might
be for mistrust to grow between the Dominion divisions and
the Higher Command. That there was such mistrust by this
time cannot be denied. The degree of demoralisation must
not be exaggerated, as it often has been since, but there is
no doubt that even those who had been spared the Battle of
Gazala, such as the New Zealanders and the recently arrived
23rd Armoured Brigade, were severely affected by their
experiences in the July battles round Ruweisat Ridge. The
problem of co-ordination and co-operation between the infantry and the armour in these battles had not been adequately
solved. This had created ill feeling on both sides. The Australians had suffered least, were fresh and in good order.
The attempt by Auchinleck, since his dismissal of Ritchie,
to combine the functions of Commander-in-Chief with those
of Army Commander in the field had been effective in bringing Rommel to a halt at El Alamein; but it had not helped
to cure this malaise.

Little wonder then that 8th Army was, in the words of
Alexander's despatch (misquoting a less flattering comment
of Winston Churchill's on the Middle East command), brave
but baffled. Clearer and clearer indications of this reached
London. Since the end of May the Chief of the Imperial
General Staff, General Sir Alan Brooke, had had to endure
daily the persistent questioning of the Prime Minister. Why,
Churchill asked, should the Army, on which so much had
been lavished, produce nothing but disaster in the only
theatres in which it was active, the Middle and the Far
East? Brooke felt it keenly and was determined to get out
to the scene of action and see for himself what was wrong.
Seizing an opportunity of finding his master in a good
mood, he had got the Prime Minister's permission on July
15th to make the journey. He laid his plans to go by way
of Gibraltar and Malta at the end of the month.

To his consternation on July 30th, the eve of his departure, Churchill told him that he had decided to go himself in order to combine a visit to Cairo and a meeting with Stalin. This development was not popular with Brooke, who had hoped to be able to form his own judgment in the freedom which would come from being on his own and away from his powerful master. He had now to move quickly if he were not to be overtaken by the Prime Minister, and in fact Brooke reached Cairo only a few hours ahead of him early in the morning of August 3rd. Field-Marshal Smuts from South Africa and General Wavell from India both arrived during the day. The Prime Minister had a long talk first with Smuts, while Brooke had an exploratory talk with General Corbett, Auchinleck's Chief of Staff at General Headquarters, before Auchinleck himself, who had come down from his desert headquarters, arrived to see the Prime Minister. Brooke was brought in later and found Churchill pressing for a resumption of attacks before September 15th, the date which Auchinleck proposed.

After dinner Brooke, longing for his bed as he had hardly slept since he left England, was to his dismay summoned for further discussion. The Prime Minister said that Auchinleck must return to Cairo and hand over command of 8th Army. This at any rate was welcome news, the very point that Brooke had himself been emphasising all along. Churchill then pressed for General Gott to take over the 8th Army.

Brooke hedged. He knew that Gott was tired. He had been in the thick of it all in the desert from the very start, rising from command of 1st Battalion King's Royal Rifle Corps in 1939 to command of 7th Armoured Division and then 13th Corps after its reverse at the hands of Rommel in January 1942. Twice, in March of 1941 and February 1942, he had been involved in trying to save the day round Tobruk, when Rommel had flung the Army out of the bulge of Cyrenaica. On his shoulders had rested the responsibility of trying to stabilise the battle round Tobruk, when the withdrawal of 8th Army from Gazala to the frontier had been forced on it in June.

These were not the only burdens he had borne. His clarity

of mind, his rock-like imperturbability and common sense, his readiness always to propose a course of action when others faltered or were in doubt, all these qualities combined with a truly Christian character had made him the oracle to whom all, both high and low, turned for advice and reassurance at all times, but especially in bad. Little wonder therefore that the strain was beginning to tell. He, like others who had been in the field since that fateful May 27th, was exhausted in body and mind.

Brooke was aware of this. He knew too that, although 'Strafer' Gott had the confidence, in many cases the devoted loyalty, of the old desert hands, there were others, particularly among the Dominion infantry divisions, who did not share this. Brooke was convinced of the need for a vigorous, fresh personality, strong-willed and self-confident. There was no doubt in his mind that Montgomery was the man. In any case he wanted to defer a decision until he had seen Gott himself. Churchill, to whom Gott had been warmly recommended by Eden, a fellow rifleman, felt that at least one figure from the old hands must be kept and was right in judging that Gott was the best of them.

When Brooke persisted in his aversion to immediate acceptance of Gott, the Prime Minister retaliated by suggesting that he himself should take over the command. The temptation to do so was naturally great, in spite of the step down from the highest position in the Army which it would entail. It was clear to him, however, that he must not accept this tempting proposal as an easy way out of his difficulties. It was therefore a very weary and exhausted Chief of the Imperial General Staff who struggled to bed in the early hours of the morning of August 4th.

He was up again in time for a long talk with Auchinleck before meeting the latter's colleagues, Admiral Sir Henry Harwood and Air-Marshal Sir Arthur Tedder. There followed a talk with Smuts before lunch with the three Commanders-in-Chief: then, in the heat of the Cairo August afternoon, a long and useful discussion with Auchinleck, at the end of which they agreed that Montgomery should take over command of 8th Army, Corbett should be replaced as Chief of Staff at General Headquarters and Gott should replace General Sir Henry Maitland Wilson, familiarly known as 'Jumbo', as Commander of British Troops in Egypt.

At a quarter to six they assembled again at the embassy for a meeting with the Prime Minister attended by Smuts and Casey, the Australian who was the British Minister of State in the Middle East. Churchill's main preoccupation was to press for an early offensive, in resisting which Brooke strongly backed the local Commanders-in-Chief. Argument was hot and long and Brooke only just had time for a bath before dinner at nine, after which the Prime Minister dragged him off into the garden.

He was not pleased at the agreement reached between Brooke and Auchinleck. It was now clear that his predilection for Gott was mainly based on the fact that he was there, knew all the facts and personalities, and was therefore available to act immediately. Appointment of Montgomery could be used as a reason for delay, whereas the Prime Minister's main concern was to hasten the moment of a new attack. The argument went on until one o'clock in the morning, leaving only three and a half hours for sleep before they were to set off for a visit to 8th Army.

In spite of his difficulties with the Prime Minister, Brooke felt he had had a good day. He was delighted and surprised that Auchinleck had been prepared to accept Montgomery. His anxiety now lay in doubts as to whether the two could work together. Auchinleck was inclined to 'breathe down the neck' of his subordinates, and this certainly would not be tolerated by Montgomery. His thoughts now turned therefore to the probable need to move Auchinleck to another command, a step which had been in the forefront of the Prime Minister's mind all along.

August 5th was an outing for all concerned, spent visiting the front at El Alamein, during which Brooke had a quiet talk with Gott who, frank and truthful as ever, himself suggested that new blood was needed, someone with new ideas and plenty of confidence in them. It was evident that Gott was tired. Brooke knew that he would never have spoken in this vein had he not been so.

This visit to 8th Army had brought Brooke first-hand confirmation of two judgments he had already formed from afar.
First that 8th Army was 'brave but baffled', in low water,
and in need both of time and of a new vigorous, tough and
determined personality before it would be ready to launch
a new offensive. Secondly that Gott, for all his great qualities and the devoted loyalty he inspired among the desert
veterans, was not the man to command it. He knew he was in
for a tough job himself in bringing both the Prime Minister
and Smuts, who had such influence on the former, round
to his view. He was prepared for this but had not expected
the attack to be launched on him before breakfast next morning, as it was.

Churchill had decided to split the Middle East Command
in two at the Suez Canal, giving the eastern half to Auchinleck and the western to Brooke himself, with Montgomery to
command 8th Army. Apart from the fact that the canal
was an impossible boundary, this would give Brooke most of
what he thought right.

This offer of the Middle East Command was a tremendous
temptation. His immediate reaction was, however, to refuse.
He knew deep down that his duty lay in facing the hardest
task of all, harnessing and guiding the tremendous drive
and energy of the Prime Minister in such a way as to keep
him on sound lines: to exploit his dynamism without
antagonising him in curbing and directing it.

Churchill used all his wiles to charm and inveigle Brooke
to accept the proposal which, but for his duty, he would
have given his all to take. Smuts was drawn in too to add his
great powers of persuasion. These two men, whose strength
of personality and qualities of eloquence swayed statesmen
and nations for half a century, could not prevail against the
devotion to duty and will-power of that stalwart soldier.

In the end the choice fell upon Alexander for the Middle
East and Gott for 8th Army. General Sir Harold Alexander,
an Irish Guardsman, had commanded a division in the
British Expeditionary Force in France at the beginning of the
war under Brooke, as Montgomery had done. From the end

of 1940 until February 1942 he had held one of the most important commands in England, Southern Command. He had then been sent to Burma just in time to face the impossible task of attempting to defend it against the Japanese. In the tragic retreat into India he had shown those qualities of imperturbability, sound judgment and common sense which Brooke had noticed at the time of Dunkirk. He had only just returned to England to command 1st Army, which was to take part in the invasion of North Africa under Eisenhower. Brooke welcomed the choice of Alexander, but still felt that the selection of Gott was wrong. He did not, however, feel so convinced about it that he must continue opposition.

That night a telegram was sent to the Cabinet seeking their approval to these changes, and recommending that Montgomery should replace Alexander in command of 1st Army. It was also recommended that Corbett should be replaced at General Headquarters and that a new commander of 30th Corps should be appointed in place of General Ramsden, the former commander of 50th Division, who had taken over from Norrie when the latter had left in July. The War Cabinet immediately agreed to the changes of command and finally gave way also on the proposal to divide the Middle East Command in two.

August 7th was a quiet day, spent by the Prime Minister in visiting the recently arrived 51st Highland Division. Before dinner that evening the tragic news arrived that Gott had been killed. He had been flying back to Cairo from Burg el Arab in a transport aircraft which was also bringing a number of soldiers and airmen. This was normally considered a safe route, so much so that it had been used two days before by the Prime Minister's own party. Two German fighters had appeared, attacked the aircraft and forced it to land in the desert. Most of its passengers, including Gott, had got out of it; but some were still trapped inside. Gott went back to help them out. A further attack set the whole aircraft ablaze and killed those inside it. It was a shock to all.

To the Prime Minister and Brooke it meant, in addition, a return to their problems. At first Churchill supported Jumbo

Wilson for the post, but Smuts agreed with Brooke and they persuaded the Prime Minister that Montgomery was the man. He must come at once, and the difficulty be faced of breaking the news to Eisenhower only twenty-four hours after the change from Alexander.

The news of these changes had yet to be broken to Auchinleck. Lieut-Colonel Ian Jacob was sent up to 8th Army Headquarters to perform this distasteful task. Auchinleck received the blow with the dignity and honesty that were characteristic of him. He refused the sop of an inactive command of the Persia-Iraq area and preferred to go. Meanwhile the Prime Minister and Brooke visited the 8th, 9th and 24th Armoured Brigades in company with Major-General Richard McCreery, whom Brooke had already suggested should be Chief of Staff to Alexander in place of Corbett.

These brigades were soon to get the new Sherman tank, which was to play so large a part in the victory of El Alamein. They had been destined for the American 1st Armoured Division, who had been eagerly awaiting them. When the news of the fall of Tobruk had come, the Prime Minister had been in conference with President Roosevelt and General Marshall in Washington. In a generous gesture of aid in adversity they had there and then diverted 300 of them to 8th Army, and the ships carrying them were now approaching Suez.

Next morning, August 9th, Alexander arrived, unfortunately for Brooke, at breakfast time. He had hoped to have a private word first, before the Prime Minister infected Alexander with suggestions as to how to fight the future battle and campaign. A few minutes only were achieved, as Churchill had already heard of his arrival. The day was spent in conference, and the Prime Minister and his party left soon after midnight on August 10th for Teheran. Before he went Churchill gave Alexander the following directive:

    1. Your prime and main duty will be to take or destroy at the earliest opportunity the German-Italian army commanded by Field-Marshal Rommel, together with all its

supplies and establishments in Egypt and Libya.

2. You will discharge or cause to be discharged such other duties as pertain to your command without prejudice to the task described in paragraph 1, which must be considered paramount in His Majesty's interests.

That same night Montgomery was leaving England. On August 7th, as GOC-in-C South Eastern Command, he had been attending a large exercise in Scotland when he had been summoned back to London to be informed that he was to replace Alexander as Commander of 1st Army under Eisenhower. His briefing at the War Office had left him with some misgivings about this task, and he returned to his headquarters at Reigate ruminating on the problems to be faced, but definitely glad to take over an active army in the field. At seven o'clock next morning the War Office was on the telephone, telling him to be ready instead to go at once to Egypt to command 8th Army. This was better news. Command of the most famous British Army in contact with the enemy under a commander that he knew well and liked. No doubts now. Only time enough to find somebody to care for his son at school; not even time to say goodbye.

Alexander was not to take over from Auchinleck until August 15th, and the reason for his presence in Cairo had not yet been made public. It was to Auchinleck therefore that Montgomery had to report on his arrival on August 12th, and from whom he had to receive his orders. This was certainly an anomalous situation. Auchinleck stressed the importance of keeping in being the 8th Army, of which he was nominally in command, Ramsden acting for him. Montgomery was to go down to the desert and look round, but not to take over command until the 15th, when Auchinleck himself handed over to Alexander. If a crisis arose before then, Auchinleck would return to take over command of the Army in the field.

None of this was to Montgomery's liking. He went straight to Alexander and put to him a proposal to form a mobile reserve corps similar to Rommel's Afrika Korps. Alexander agreed, and Montgomery went on to discuss it with General John Harding, one of the Deputy Chiefs of Staff at General Headquarters, the only member of the General Staff hierarchy who was to stay. Harding promised that he could produce such a corps, which could consist of the New Zealand Division, the 1st and either the 8th or the 10th Armoured Division: it would be called 10th Corps and would take over this role from 30th Corps, which had been formed before Operation 'Crusader' in September 1941 as an armoured corps for the same purpose.

At five o'clock in the morning of August 13th Montgomery left Cairo by car for the desert. He was met, where the coast road joins the desert road to Alexandria, by Brigadier Freddie de Guingand, who was then Brigadier General Staff of 8th Army. He was an old acquaintance and it was not long before Montgomery had persuaded him to give his views frankly and openly about the unsatisfactory state of 8th Army. During the drive along the coast road Montgomery decided to take him as his Chief of Staff, a relationship that was to endure until the end of the war.

They arrived at 8th Army Headquarters at about eleven. Montgomery did not like the look of it. It had too temporary and dismal an air. Ramsden was there and Montgomery cross-questioned him about the plans. By the time he had finished, Montgomery had decided that he could not tolerate two days hanging about under these conditions. He therefore told Ramsden to return to his corps, having decided in spite of Auchinleck's orders to assume command immediately. Ramsden submitted in surprise. During a fly-ridden, shade-less lunch Montgomery decided to go further and counter-manded all orders for withdrawal. At two o'clock he sent a signal to General Headquarters to say what he had done, after which he left the Headquarters to visit 13th Corps, hoping to be out in case of a come-back. Freyberg, re-covered from his wounds, had temporarily taken over com-mand of 13th Corps when Gott had been killed. In him Montgomery found a sympathetic ear for the ideas which he had already formed. He got back to 8th Army Head-quarters at half past six, and immediately addressed the staff which had been assembled.

He explained his intention. There was to be no withdrawal. The Army would hold its present line, send transport to the rear and store supplies in the forward area. To make this possible more troops would be brought forward from the Delta. Egypt would be defended at El Alamein and not behind it. A new Reserve Armoured Corps was to be formed. Divisions must be fought as divisions and not split up. Finally Army Headquarters itself must be made comfortable and must therefore move to the sea; it must be close to the Air Force Headquarters. He had been ordered to destroy Rommel and his army. If Rommel attacked soon, it might be tricky: in a week it would be all right: in two weeks' time he would be seen off. Whatever happened Montgomery himself would not attack until he was ready. De Guingand was to be his Chief of Staff and had complete authority over the head-quarters and all branches of the staff. Any orders from him were to be regarded as the commander's own orders and obeyed instantly.

The next day was given over to consideration of what to do if Rommel attacked in the near future as he was expected to do.

First of all Montgomery considered the picture of the enemy, who also had been digging and laying minefields. The northern sector was commanded by Lieutenant-General Navarini's XXI Italian Corps. The front line from the coast to Deir el Shein was held by the recently arrived German 164th Division superimposed on the Italian Trento Division: from Deir el Shein to a few miles north-east of Qaret el Abd by the Italian Bologna Division. The southern sector was the responsibility of Lieutenant-General Orsi's X Italian Corps. North of Gebel Kalakh was the Italian Brescia Division with battalions of the German Colonel Ramcke's Special 288 Parachute Brigade interspersed among them. South of that, covering the area between Gebel Kalakh, the Taqa plateau and Naqb abu Dweis, was the Italian Folgore Parachute Division. In reserve behind were the two mobile corps, Major General de Stefanis' XX Italian Corps with Ariete Armoured Division behind Brescia north-west of Qaret el Abd, Littorio Division behind Folgore, just west of Gebel Kalakh, and Trieste, the Motorised Division, a few miles to the north-west.

Of the Germans, 21st Panzer Division was in the north, about six miles north-west of Deir el Shein, and 15th Panzer Division was in the centre, about the same distance north-west of Qaret el Abd. 90th Light Division was in process of being relieved in the front line and was concentrating between Ariete and Littorio west of Qaret el Abd.

The indications were that Rommel was preparing his mobile corps for a fresh attack. It was thought likely that he would aim to deliver it near the period of the full moon, which fell on August 26th. As he was mining in the northern sector as intensely as we were, it was thought likely that he would, as usual, try a bold sweep round the southern flank and cut up to the coast.

The plan which Montgomery found in existence to meet the threat was that 30th Corps on the right should hold firmly the position occupied in succession by 9th Australian, 1st South African and 5th Indian Divisions from Tel el Eisa south-eastwards to the edge of the El Alamein 'box', and then south to include Ruweisat Ridge. In reserve behind these divisions was 23rd Armoured Brigade with Valentine tanks. South of Ruweisat Ridge the New Zealand Division under 13th Corps had two brigades holding positions extending down to Bare Ridge. They also had under their command 21st Indian Infantry Brigade at Alam el Halfa, in place of their own 4th Brigade which was reorganising near Cairo. There was therefore a large gap on Bare Ridge between the New Zealand Division's forward brigades and the Indian Brigade at Alam el Halfa.

Also under 13th Corps was 7th Armoured Division. It had 22nd Armoured Brigade near Alam el Halfa, 7th Motor Brigade patrolling the minefields between the New Zealanders on Bare Ridge and Himeimat and 4th Light Armoured Brigade which kept a motor battalion round Himeimat and operated armoured cars west of the minefields by day and also south of Himeimat.

The Dominion divisions on the whole were in pretty good order, but 5th Indian Division and 7th Armoured Division were still rather a jumble of units, not yet fully sorted out since their arrival in the El Alamein Line and the battles all through July. As far as equipment went, the Army was not in too bad a shape. There were close on 600 tanks, of which over 400 were with units and fit for battle. Field artillery was up to strength with 20 guns a regiment, but there were only two medium regiments with a total of 26 guns between them. There was a serious shortage of anti-tank guns, especially the new 6-pounders; but during the month many infantry battalions received their first 2-pounders as the artillery anti-tank regiments got their 6-pounders.

Some important aspects of defensive battles in the desert had impressed Auchinleck and his staff. First, that there was no point in putting too many infantry in defensive positions, if there was not enough anti-tank and field artillery with them to provide an effective all-round defence. Second, that static positions alone were useless. It was essential to be able to move and concentrate the greatest possible amount of fire-power wherever the enemy himself concentrated to attack. A balance had to be maintained therefore between the troops, particularly the artillery, committed to defensive positions and those kept available to move. Third, that all the various units and headquarters needed in the immediate rear of the battle must not be stampeded by the irruption of the enemy's mobile force into that area. They must therefore be capable of holding out for a period, if this happened, until the action of our own mobile forces cleared the area again. To this end they must be grouped and organised into localities for self-defence. Finally that, if the enemy succeeded in penetrating even further into the rear, means must exist both to protect and also to evacuate the large numbers of immobile and generally defenceless administrative troops and installations in the area.

Appreciation of these needs led Auchinleck to order that defensive positions should normally consist of 'boxes' to hold two infantry battalions and a battery each of field, anti-tank and light anti-aircraft artillery. Outside these the remainder of the division's forces should be organised in mobile groups, which could move and concentrate against the enemy. In the rear areas of divisions and in the area of Corps and Army Headquarters there was to be a total of ten localities (or boxes) in which all other units were to be organised for self-defence. Behind this, again, reserve positions were to be prepared near Amiriya and the Wadi Natrun, covering the forward airfield area. There were plans for some defensive works and flooding in the Delta itself, and for patrolling the desert between Cairo and Siwa, but these were not the concern of 8th Army.

If, as was expected, Rommel attacked in the south and tried to sweep right round behind 30th Corps positions, the plan was for 13th Corps to refuse the left flank on the line of Bare Ridge back to Alam el Halfa, just as the intention had been in May to do the same from Bir Hacheim to Bir el Gubi. The problem remained that there were not enough troops to do this without committing the only effective mobile forces, 7th Armoured Division, to filling the gap between the New Zealand Division's forward position on Bare Ridge and 21st Indian Infantry Brigade at Alam el Halfa. The Commander of 7th Armoured Division, General Renton, who had himself been commanding 7th Motor Brigade on May 27th in a position very similar to that in which the same brigade now were, had bitter memories of the difficulty of getting both the motor and the armoured brigades into position in time. He preferred to withdraw them eastwards to the south of Alam el Halfa in order to be able to strike Rommel on the outer right flank when he wheeled north, wherever that might be.

There were several features of this plan which Montgomery did not like. Above all he disliked the fact that the whole concept was based on the premise that Rommel's mobile forces would penetrate round and behind the forward defensive positions. He was immediately impressed with the importance of Ruweisat Ridge: this must be firmly held. When he came to consider the southern sector of 13th Corps, where the real problem lay, he quickly realised two essentials. First, the importance of the Alam el Halfa area. Secondly that, with only a fairly small addition to the forces available to him, he could have enough both to hold securely the refused flank of Bare Ridge and also to keep a mobile force ready to strike Rommel on the flank or to meet him if he moved even wider. He knew that such forces were in fact available in the Delta both from recent arrivals and from those in the process of reorganising. He saw no reason why considerable risks should be run on the vital battle-field while these troops were available only a short distance away. Once he had them, there would be no need for all this peculiar box business and all this anxiety about the rear areas. Apart from being unfamiliar, it was untidy and obviously unpopular.

As has been related, his first steps were devoted to strengthening the forward defences and to cancelling all measures which threw doubt on the possibility of holding them firmly. He then quickly applied himself to the task of filling the gaps in the southern sector of 13th Corps. That very evening, the 14th, de Guingand was made to ring up General Headquarters and demand the immediate despatch of 44th (Home Counties) Division, which it was planned to move up at the end of the month. The staff in Cairo said that they would try and get some part of it moving in a few days' time, but that it could not be complete earlier than planned. When de Guingand reported this, Montgomery immediately rang Harding. The latter put Montgomery's request first to Corbett, then to Auchinleck and finally to Alexander. All agreed that every effort would be made to meet Montgomery's wishes and the division arrived on the 16th, one of its brigades following a day later. Its 132nd brigade was put under command of the New Zealand Division and completed their position forward on Bare Ridge. The rest of the division relieved 21st Indian Brigade at Alam el Halfa and set to work immediately to strengthen and extend the position.

At the same time Lieutenant-General Brian Horrocks arrived to take over command of 13th Corps. He had been specially asked for by Montgomery, who had admired his restless and energetic enthusiasm in South Eastern Command in England. Forty-six years old, he had been captured wounded when serving with his regiment, the Middlesex, in the First World War. At the outbreak of the Second he was commanding their 2nd battalion in France. Since May 1940 he had commanded a brigade, been Brigadier General

Staff to Eastern Command, and commanded both 44th Infantry and 9th Armoured Division, all in England. He was highly strung, almost fanatically enthusiastic and could turn on suave charm or biting anger with equal facility.

Within the next ten days 8th Army was reinforced with artillery and tanks. Headquarters 10th Armoured Division (Gatehouse) came up with 8th Armoured Brigade (Custance). At the same time efforts were made to mislead the enemy. First of all he was to be led into deferring his attack altogether by an impression of great strength in the south. Two dummy tank battalions were moved into the area east of Himeimat, a dummy infantry brigade position was dug at Samaket Gaballa and dummy minefields were also laid. All this was completed by August 25th. If in spite of this Rommel were to break through, he was to be misled as to the nature of the 'going' by a false 'going' map deliberately lost on patrol in the forward area. There was in fact an area of very soft sand south of Alam el Halfa: this was shown as good hard 'going', and the good 'going' shown as bad in the hope of luring Rommel into that area. Unfortunately for those who planned to deceive, there is no sign that any of these measures had any effect on Rommel's plans or even came to his notice, certainly not the first.

By the time of the full moon therefore 8th Army was in much better trim to meet Rommel. 30th Corps' (Ramsden) orders were to hold all its positions to the last man and the last round. 13th Corps' (Horrocks) plan was that the positions held by the New Zealand Division (Freyberg) and 44th Division (Hughes) were also to be held and fought to the last man and round. 7th Armoured Division (Renton), responsible for the front south of the New Zealanders, was if possible to stop the enemy on the forward minefields. If this were not possible, they were to delay and harass him as much as they possibly could. To do this they had 7th Motor Brigade (Bosvile) and 4th Light Armoured Brigade (Carr), which had very few tanks and those all Stuarts or Crusaders. The division's own armoured brigade, the 22nd (Roberts), had been removed and placed under 10th Armoured Division. Gatehouse therefore had two armoured brigades, the 22nd, positioned just west of Alam el Halfa round Point 102, and the 8th who were 6 miles to the south-east of Alam el Halfa and therefore 10 miles east of Roberts. Hughes' infantry positions were between the two brigades and slightly in rear of them. Gatehouse's command was designated as Corps reserve and was to be prepared either to occupy battle positions in the areas in which the brigades were, or to be launched in a counter-attack by Horrocks, possibly with Richards' 23rd Armoured Brigade from 30th Corps as well.

Army Headquarters had moved on August 16th to a pleasant site by the sea near Burg el Arab, where it was close to the headquarters of Air-Marshal Coningham's Desert Air Force. Together they planned that, when Rommel attacked, his concentrations of vehicles would be bombed by night by Wellingtons of the RAF and Albacores of the Fleet Air Arm, who would also drop flares to find and mark the targets. By day every available aircraft would participate, Boston light bombers also attacking the airfield at Daba and Rommel's headquarters which was thought to be near by.

Full moon came on the 26th, but no attack. Everybody was kept at a high state of readiness and alert. As the days passed, the moon began to wane and still no attack came. The professional deceivers began to think that they had done their job and frightened him off.

As soon as Tobruk had fallen to him on June 21st, Rommel, now a Field Marshal, proposed that the plan to limit his advance to the frontier should be abandoned and that, with the supplies captured in Tobruk in his hands, he should exploit to the utmost the confusion his victory had caused. He would head straight for Alexandria and Cairo and the speed of his advance would prevent the British from recovering sufficiently to organise any resistance.

Rommel, as Commander of the German and Italian Panzer Armee Afrika, came under the orders of the Italian High Command, the Comando Supremo, headed by Marshal Cavallero, to which General von Rintelen was attached as representative of the German High Command, the OKW. In Italy also was Field-Marshal Kesselring, commander of all the German air forces in the Mediterranean, to whom Rommel was officially subordinate in the purely German chain of command. In practice Rommel received orders direct from the OKW. These were very often at variance with the orders of the Italians. Although he often complained about the situation, Rommel in fact exploited it to his own advantage.

Before his attack at Gazala at the end of May, Rommel had proposed that it was essential to deal with Malta first. Operation 'Hercules' had been planned for this, but was clearly not going to be carried out in time, although it had been in preparation since February. It had finally been agreed that it would take place immediately after Rommel's attempt to recapture Tobruk. The air forces needed would then be switched to deal with Malta.

Both the Italians and Kesselring opposed Rommel's request to dash headlong for the Nile. Their resources would not be able to support his forces more than 300 miles beyond Tobruk and 700 from Benghazi as well as reducing Malta. If the latter were not dealt with, it would make the maintenance of Rommel's force in Egypt a hazardous affair.

Rommel's own chief operational staff officer, Colonel Siegfried Westphal, shared these prudent views.

Rommel regarded this prudence as pusillanimous. Here was a great opportunity to capture the key area of the Middle East and link up with the German armies north of the Caucasus. Cautious and gloomy prognostications about difficulties of air support and supply should be disregarded, as they had been on both occasions on which he had thrust forward from El Agheila. He would be in the Nile Delta before the British could reorganise: all the resources of their vast base with its airfields would then be at his disposal. Their Navy and Air Force would no longer be able to operate in the Eastern Mediterranean, and the difficulties which had beset his supply line from Italy would disappear.

Hitler, who had never in any case been in favour of the Malta operation, backed Rommel and overbore the objections of the Comando Supremo. Rommel, flinging caution to the winds, sped for the Nile.

As has been related, he failed in his first wild fling. The almost continuous series of battles throughout July quickly used up the supplies captured at Tobruk. The ammunition was, of course, only of use for captured guns. By the end of July, when both sides paused, his logistic situation was already critical. As a port Tobruk alone could only handle 600 tons a day, a minute fraction of his needs, and was in any case very vulnerable to air attack. Both Benghazi and Tripoli had to be used too. There was no means of making use of the railway between Tobruk and the front, although attempts were made to do so. It took twelve days for lorries to do the trip to the front and back from Tripoli, seven from Benghazi. Rommel was short of transport. Most of what he had was captured and, because there were no spares for it, a very large proportion was always unserviceable. To make matters worse, the reinforcements he had received, German parachutists from Crete, 164th Division and Colonel Ramcke's Special Group 288, and the Italian Folgore Parachute Division had all come by air and had brought no vehicles with them.

This problem of vehicles and of supply was Rommel's greatest worry. He now blamed those who had foreseen these difficulties for not bestirring themselves to make super-human efforts to get across to him the vehicles, equipment and stores which he knew existed in Italy and Germany. But in face of naval and air attacks from Malta and from bases in Egypt, both the journey across the Mediterranean, now longer than before, and unloading in the battered ports of Cyrenaica, had become costly and dangerous operations. Only 6,000 tons were landed in July, one-fifth of the quota planned. In the first three weeks of August, although no operations of any importance took place, the Panzer Armee Afrika used up almost double the supplies which were brought across the Mediterranean in the same period. To add insult to injury, at the beginning of August the Italians sent over the Pistoia Division with three or four hundred vehicles to Libya. The division was not to be used in Egypt, and this at a time when the German 164th Division in the front line had only sixty vehicles. Not one replacement for the Germans left Italy in July.

Rommel made bitter complaints to the Italians and to Kesselring. He pointed out that the forces in Libya contained about two Germans for every Italian, 82,000 to 42,000; but in August the German Army only received 8,200 tons, barely a third of its needs, while the Italians got three times that amount and even the German Air Force, who seemed unable to be effective, got more than the Army.

It is difficult, so long after the event, to be sure of the truth of Rommel's complaints. What we do know is that 30 freight ships, 14 barges and 6 submarines were despatched from Italy to arrive in North Africa in August, and that, of these, 4 ships were sunk by submarine and 3 by air attack en route; 14 ships, 13 barges and 2 submarines came to Tobruk; 7 ships and 2 submarines to Benghazi; one of each to Tripoli; and one submarine to Derna. Of the 3,720 tons of ammunition sent, 1,660 were lost: of 15,500 tons of petrol and oil, 2,700 were lost: of 6,370 tons of general supplies and equipment, 2,120 were lost: 43 out of 220 guns and 367 out of 1,147 vehicles were lost: all 39 tanks sent arrived. In spite of the fact that losses of petrol were smaller in proportion than of any other item, the Panzer Armee was using it up so fast that it was the main cause of worry.

On top of these troubles about his logistics came a further source of anxiety – sickness. Health and hygiene was not one of the strong points of the Panzer Armee Afrika. A large proportion of the officers and men had been in action continuously for two and a half years. The strain of the pace at which Rommel drove them all, including himself, was now beginning to tell. There was a high proportion of sickness and a general lassitude once the flush of the victorious race into Egypt was over. Rommel himself was sick and was subject to frequent attacks of fainting. His doctor, Professor Hörster, diagnosed it as a combination of chronic stomach and intestinal catarrh, nasal diphtheria and considerable circulation trouble. His Chief of Staff, General Gause, was subject to violent headaches and Colonel Westphal was shortly to go down with jaundice.

Worries about the state of the Army were not therefore confined to the British. While greatly concerned at his own logistic problems and the difficulties of building up an effective force, Rommel realised that his opponents, back almost in their base area with a short line of communication, had a distinct advantage. He appreciated that by now reinforcements and supplies from England and America would be on the way and might be available at the front within a very short time of landing at Suez. The visit of Churchill showed the importance which the British attached to holding on to Egypt. German intelligence estimated that a large convoy, carrying well over 100,000 tons of equipment and stores would reach Suez before the beginning of September. It was essential for Rommel to strike again before 8th Army could make use of this. The latest possible date would be at the period of the full moon which fell on August 26th.

But this was not the only consideration favouring an early attack. Every day that passed saw a strengthening of the British defences, particularly in the laying and thickening of minefields. There was now practically no hope of achieving a rapid break-through in the northern half of the line, from the coast to Ruweisat Ridge. The defences and minefields were being extended southwards. Every day that passed reduced the possibility of a swift move to envelop 8th Army and then throw it off balance, the stratagem that had succeeded so many times before. Once effective minefields, backed by even fairly lightly held defences, could be extended to Qaret el Himeimat, the possibility of this would disappear. An attack then would be a head-on affair, in which the material abundance and the dogged persistence of 8th Army in defence would tilt the balance increasingly in their favour. The one hope of success lay in forcing a mobile battle on the British in which they would be unable, because of the uncertainty of the situation and the normally slow reaction of their command, to bring their superior fire-power including their air power to bear.

The earliest possible date was called for, but nothing could be done until the supply situation, particularly the petrol situation, improved. Rommel never ceased badgering Kesselring and Cavallero. His state of health accentuated his normally direct manner, and relations between Rommel and the Italians became acutely strained.

With the full moon on August 26th as his target date, Rommel set himself to consider the plan for his attack. The battles of July and the increasing strength of the defences ruled out any hope of an easy break-through on Ruweisat Ridge or north of it.

South of the Ridge and north of the depressions running south-east from Qaret el Abd, 8th Army were busy digging, blasting and laying mines. By the end of the month the chances of being able to stage a rapid break-through here would be slender too.

The sector south of the depressions and north of the escarpment running from Gebel Kalakh to Himeimat was held by 7th Armoured Division, his old opponents. They were up to their usual tricks of patrolling well forward with armoured cars and small columns of motor infantry, backed by guns. It made it difficult for Rommel to find out himself what was going on there, but he thought it unlikely that defensive activity would be very intense. Air reconnaissance showed that the area was very lightly held. To lay too many mines would only limit the ability of 8th Army's own armoured forces to make a counter-thrust when their turn came.

Rommel therefore decided to repeat almost exactly the plan which had brought him such success on May 27th south of Tobruk. Everything was to be staked on a very rapid thrust during the night round, as he thought, 8th Army's southern flank north of Himeimat. Before dawn Nehring's Afrika Korps, 15th and 21st Panzer Divisions, was to be south of Alam el Halfa right round the rear of 8th Army's position. Their right flank was to be covered by a group formed from all the German and Italian reconnaissance units. On their left would be de Stefanis' XX Corps, Ariete and Littorio Armoured Divisions. Further to the left still, moving through the depressions, would come Kleemann's German 90th Light Division. By half past three in the morning they were all to be in position facing north.

As soon as it was light the Afrika Korps was to advance rapidly northwards to the coast near Ruweisat station, while the formations on its left made shorter 'hooks' into the rear of the British positions about Ruweisat Ridge. 8th Army would be surrounded and completely cut off from supply. Their airfields, supply area and Alexandria itself would be immediately threatened, and nothing would stand between Rommel and Cairo. Once he had reached the coast Nehring was to turn east into the British supply area. Rommel appreciated that this would force 8th Army to move back its mobile forces, which he was confident he could defeat in a fluid battle. The defensive positions near El Alamein could then be dealt with at leisure by his infantry divisions, as Tobruk had been dealt with in June, while his mobile divisions dashed on to Alexandria, Cairo and beyond. Von Bismarck's Panzer Division was to outflank Alexandria on the south. Von Vaerst's 15th Panzer and Kleemann's 90th Light were to drive straight through the desert to Cairo, where they were to be relieved by the Italian Mobile Corps, travelling by Wadi Natrun and the desert road. Von Vaerst and Kleemann were then to go on to Suez, while de Stefanis pursued the remnants of the British up the Nile Valley.

Three things were essential for this plan to succeed. Surprise, speed and the supplies to fight a mobile battle. To gain surprise it would be vital to conceal to the very last the move of his mobile forces to the south. The tanks were to be moved by night into hiding places in broken ground near Gebel Kalakh, where they could remain camouflaged by day. This would be done over a period of four nights, a quarter of the tanks moving on each night. The wheeled vehicles were to make the move to the assembly area in one bound the night before the attack was to be launched. Their absence from their previous area was to be concealed by moving up supply units to take their place. To help surprise, a diversionary attack was to be made on Ruweisat Ridge slightly before the main attack in the south.

Speed was to be obtained by simultaneous movement on a broad front, brushing aside the light resistance expected and pushing forward boldly in spite of casualties which the odd minefield might cause. Rommel had little fear on this score. The Afrika Korps could be relied on to thrust forward boldly, but a full moon was essential and that would not fall until the 26th.

His one doubt was supply, above all petrol. The ability to press on the first morning, to force a mobile battle on the enemy and to exploit the confusion he would cause rested on petrol and the assurance of its supply until he reached the British forward base.

There was no sign of the arrival of the petrol Rommel needed. As he saw time slipping away his anxiety aggravated his already poor state of health. On August 22nd, Rommel represented to von Rintelen the minimum demands which he said were essential if he were to launch the attack, which could not be postponed beyond the end of the month. These included the assurance of certain minimum stocks of petrol and ammunition, the latter to be at least four days' supply, over and above that held by units. On the 27th, when the full moon had already arrived, Kesselring flew to see him. Rommel's complaints were bitter. In the end he extracted a promise from his superior that in a situation of extreme crisis Kesselring would send over 500 tons a day by air.

As the last days of the month went by and the moon

began to wane, there was no sign of the petrol or the ammunition which Comando Supremo had promised. Rommel knew that, if he did not attack, all his hopes of defeating 8th Army, and indeed his chances of avoiding defeat himself, would pass. By the next full moon a rapid break-through would be impossible and 8th Army would have in the field the reinforcements and equipment that must, even now, be travelling up the Red Sea. Rommel had ordered the assembly of the tanks to start as soon as Kesselring had left. Any further delay might prejudice surprise. On August 28th Rommel summoned his Corps Commanders, with von Vaerst, von Bismarck and Kleemann, to give them his final orders for the attack, now to take place on the night of August 30th. Confirmation of this order, however, depended on the arrival of three petrol tankers within the next two days. The tank strength of the army, as reported to him, was as follows: the Germans had 26 of the new Mark IV Specials with the long 75-mm. gun, and 10 of the old ones with the short 75-mm.: 71 of the new Mark III (J)s with the long 50-mm. and 93 of the old ones with the shorter gun: a total of exactly 200 tanks, not counting 29 light and 5 command tanks. The Italians had 243 of their medium tanks and 38 light tanks.

In response to a final desperate appeal from Rommel, Cavallero informed him on August 30th that tankers full of petrol would arrive under escort at Tobruk and Benghazi within a few hours, at the latest on the next day. That day also Kesselring transferred to Rommel 1,500 tons of Air Force petrol. This gave him his four days' supply in addition to the two or three days' supply with units. Certain of only a week's petrol, but with the somewhat slender assurance of more in the offing, Rommel gave the order for the attack to be launched as planned that night. The die was cast. Everything he had was at stake.

4 ALAM EL HALFA

August 31st – September 7th

The moon, five days past full, was due to rise twenty minutes before midnight, an hour earlier by the time the Germans and Italians were keeping. Nearly two hours before this Rommel's columns began to make their way forward from the area between Qaret el Abd and Gebel Kalakh. It came as a shock to them when shortly afterwards a heavy air raid began on the area north-west of Kalakh, where a great deal of their transport was assembled. The Royal Air Force had spotted it moving there the previous night, in spite of the attempts of the Luftwaffe to prevent them. This sowed the first seed of doubt about the attack coming as a surprise.

At the same time as they began to move forward, the Germans started to shell the gaps in the minefields which they had spotted 7th Armoured Division's patrols using. This aroused the suspicions of the units concerned. 2nd Battalion The Rifle Brigade held the area south of the New Zealanders on Bare Ridge down to the depression of Deir el Munassib, where 2nd Battalion King's Royal Rifle Corps (60th) took over. South of the depression the composite regiment of 10th Hussars which had a company of the Rifle Brigade under their command, looked after the two parallel minefields down to about half-way between Munassib and Himeimat. South of that Carr's 4th Light Armoured Brigade was responsible with 1st Battalion 60th backed by the composite regiment of 4th/8th Hussars.

At about the time the moon rose, reports began to come in from these forward troops of the noise of movement to the west of them. It was not long before the enemy's leading troops reached the edge of the first minefield and began to try and lift the mines, but by this time everybody was ready for them. The machine-guns and mortars of the Green-jackets opened up and all the guns of the 3rd and 4th Regi-ments Royal Horse Artillery which could reach began to fire. Half an hour later the picture began to come clearer. In the north, on the front of 2nd Rifle Brigade, 18 tanks had come forward to support the enemy infantry, but the Rifle Brigade opened fire with their 6-pounders and stopped them. While F Battery RHA put down a 'stonk', the carriers counter-attacked and drove the enemy infantry back.

In Munassib itself 90th Light Division tried to pick up the mines on the front of 2nd/60th. The same tactics were repeated here with success. South of the depression 10th Hussars reported no serious attack, but in 1st/60th's sector, just north of Himeimat, the Afrika Korps were trying to force their way through.

The pattern of attack was now clear and 7th Armoured Division passed it on to Corps and Army with a request for the RAF to get busy between the minefields and Gebel Kalakh. At the same time they moved the dummy tanks back out of harm's way. The aircraft, Wellingtons and Albacores, back from their previous raid, bombed up again and returned. As they dropped their flares on the mass of vehicles below, Rommel's forward troops were silhouetted for the benefit of the Greenjackets.

The Panzer Armee had expected a clear drive through with only a short halt to pick up a few odd mines. They were not prepared for a methodical attack to capture the area of the minefields and clear wide gaps through several in succession. By the time they should have been lined up facing north from Alam el Halfa to Bare Ridge, refuelled and ready for the dawn thrust to the coast, they still had not penetrated the first minefield. To Rommel's insistent telephone enquiries they replied that opposition was much heavier and the minefields much more intricate than expected. They had already suffered considerable casualties. To the Greenjackets it seemed that the Germans were not attacking with anything like their normal vigour.

The first strong renewed thrust was made by the Afrika Korps just north of Himeimat soon after half past four, with about an hour's darkness to go, when they finally made a large breach in the first minefield. About 60 tanks got through and began to bring considerable pressure to bear on the

second minefield. Immediately to the north the 10th Hussars
were now worried about their left flank. They asked for and
received permission to withdraw to the second minefield. This
made the position of 2nd/60th to the north of them in Munassib an anxious one, particularly as shortly afterwards 90th
Light Division with 30 tanks finally broke through the first
minefield in the depression itself on the boundary between
the 2nd/60th and 2nd Rifle Brigade. Six tanks were knocked
out but the rest moved on eastwards. Bosvile now feared
that the enemy might reach the gaps in the second minefield,
which was only lightly defended, before he could get his
riflemen back through them. He therefore ordered them to
come back to the second minefield, which they succeeded in
doing by half past seven. 10th Hussars were then also behind
it with one squadron facing south a little further east.

By this time, after more than an hour's daylight, Carr's
brigade had had to relinquish their hold on Himeimat and
were harrying the enemy from the escarpment to the south
of them while withdrawing the bulk of 1st/60th to Samaket
Gaballa. The task of hanging on to the escarpment and
delaying the enemy as much as possible was given to 4th/8th
Hussars, who started the day with 50 of the American Stuart
light tanks, then known as 'Honeys'. Back at Samaket Gaballa
was the 3rd County of London Yeomanry, the Sharpshooters,
with only 27 Crusaders, one of their squadrons being away
serving with their sister regiment, 4th County of London
Yeomanry, in Roberts' 22nd Armoured Brigade.

Rommel was at Gebel Kalakh at eight o'clock, where he
received a gloomy report on the progress of the attack on
which all his hopes were pinned. Progress had been very slow.
Shortly after passing the eastern edge of their own minefields
his forces had come up against what they called 'an extremely
strong and hitherto unsuspected British mine belt, stubbornly
defended, thick with booby traps and covered by heavy fire'.
These, together with incessant heavy air attacks, had caused
many casualties. General Nehring, the Commander of the
Afrika Korps, had been wounded in an air attack, and General
von Bismarck, Commander of 21st Panzer Division, killed
by a mine.

None of the conditions, surprise, speed and supply, had been fulfilled. Rommel seriously considered abandoning the whole operation. He came to the conclusion that his decision would depend on the prospects of the Afrika Korps, the command of which had been taken over temporarily by Colonel Bayerlein, then Chief of Staff. Rommel went on to see Bayerlein, who reported that he had just suceeded in breaking through the minefield belt near Himeimat and begged to be allowed to go on. Rommel agreed, but changed the original plan to make his forces turn north sooner. The Afrika Korps would now have Alam el Halfa itself as their objective instead of moving to the east of it. This would give de Stefanis the area round Point 102 as his objective. with Kleemann on his left. It was not a cheerful prospect for Rommel, sick man as he was.

The situation reported to Montgomery at the same time was a cheering one. 30th Corps had had a fairly uneventful night except on Ruweisat Ridge, where 2nd West Yorks in 5th Indian Division had been fiercely attacked by Ramcke's parachutists and lost one whole company. However the situation had been restored at first light. 164th Division had raided the Australians, while the South Africans had raided Trento about the same time as the latter were about to raid them, and had the best of the encounter. The New Zealanders had not been attacked and a fighting patrol of their 18th Battalion had captured 30 Bersaglieri from Brescia.

On 13th Corps' front the enemy had clearly launched three main thrusts: the first immediately south of the New Zealanders, the second in Munassib, and the most southerly just north of Himeimat. It was not yet clear just how strong a force was involved, but it was certain that at least one of the two German Panzer divisions and 90th Light were engaged, and it also looked as if at least part of XX Corps was in it too. There was a hope that the whole thing might be brought to a halt on the minefields in 7th Armoured Division's area. If not, the reserves round Alam el Halfa were ready to meet whatever came.

In the next hour and a half the Afrika Korps' thrust from Himeimat was the main event. It included at least 100 tanks and had soon shaken free of the second minefield. The recon-

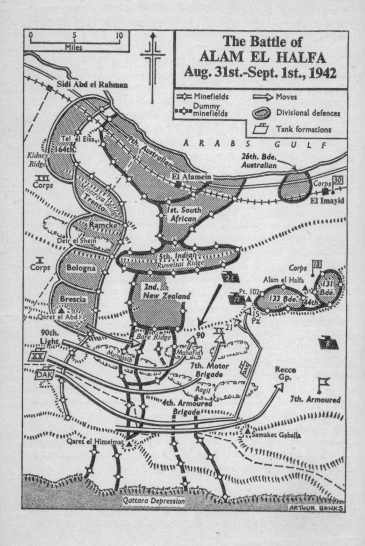

The Battle of
ALAM EL HALFA
Aug. 31st.–Sept. 1st., 1942

Minefields
Dummy minefields
Moves
Divisional defences
Tank formations

Scale: 0 — 5 — 10 Miles

Sidi Abd el Rahman

A R A B S   G U L F

Tel el Eisa

9th. Australian

164th.

Kidney Ridge

El Alamein

26th. Bde. Australian

XXX Corps

Corps 30

El Imayid

Mersha Trench

1st. South African

Ramcke

Deir el Shein

5th. Indian
Ruweisat Ridge

Corps 13

X Corps

Bologna

2nd. New Zealand

Alam el Halfa

131 Bde.

Pc. 102

133 Bde.

44th.

Brescia

23

22

Qaret el Abd

15 Pz.

90th. Light

Bare Ridge

90

XXX 21

8

Mungssib

Munafid

7th. Motor Brigade

DAK

DAK

Recce Gp.

Ragil

7th. Armoured

4th. Armoured Brigade

Samaket Gaballa

Qaret el Himeimat

Qattara Depression

ARTHUR BANKS

naissance units began to push Carr off the escarpment to the south, and the eastward move of this considerable force of enemy tanks south of Ragil caused concern to Bosvile and particularly to the 10th Hussars, although there was in fact little direct pressure on their front. It seems that de Stefanis and Kleemann found the difficulties of organising their movement through the minefields and confused escarpments on the edges of the various depressions quite enough to hold them up, although they protested to Rommel that they were strongly opposed. In fact it was the fear of his troops getting cut off and surrounded among the minefields rather than direct enemy pressure which caused Bosvile to bring all his forward troops back to the area of his reserve battalion, 7th Rifle Brigade, north of the eastern end of Ragil, by about half past nine. By this time Bayerlein had just reached the final minefield in Carr's area, seven miles east of Himeimat.

When this movement was reported to Horrocks, he reacted strongly. This was not his interpretation of the orders he had given to Renton to stop the enemy if possible on the forward minefield: if not, to impose the maximum delay. He considered that the old hands attached too much importance to keeping the forces in being instead of offering the maximum resistance. He ordered the division to hold the line of the final minefield which Bosvile had already left. Renton protested against the confusion that this would cause, but was overborne, and the 10th Hussars were sent back again. They set off about mid-day and took up a position in the depression north-east of Munassib, known as Muhafid, facing south and in touch with the New Zealand divisional cavalry in that area. At the same time Richards' 23rd Armoured Brigade, leaving behind one squadron from each regiment with the divisions of 30th Corps, was transferred to 13th Corps and moved down to Bare Ridge between the New Zealanders and 22nd Armoured Brigade, arriving at a quarter past one and coming under command of Gatehouse.

Rommel cannot have been very happy about the progress of his army by mid-day, more than twenty-four hours after they had started. Ramcke's brigade with the Bersaglieri of

Brescia were still in the area between the minefields which 2nd Rifle Brigade had defended south of the New Zealanders. In XX Corps, Ariete Armoured Division and Trieste Motor Division were just south of Munassib where 10th Hussars had been. Littorio Armoured Division was a few miles to the south-east, south of the western end of Ragil. The Afrika Korps with 21st Panzer to the north and 15th Panzer Division to the south was halted to refuel a few miles west of Samaket Gaballa with the reconnaissance units further south. Air attacks had been continuous, but from half past eleven a dust storm began to blow up from the south, which both helped to conceal the forces and also prevented aircraft from taking off.

At half past twelve de Guingand telephoned to Brigadier Erskine, Chief of Staff of 13th Corps. The latter told him that Bosvile's situation was confused. There had been a report of 73 tanks in the area, but the New Zealanders denied this and the brigade had been ordered back into the area. Renton thought that the enemy might be intending to move between Ragil and Samaket Gaballa. There had been reports of Italian tanks, but they had not been confirmed. It was still not certain if both 15th and 21st Panzer Divisions were engaged.

An hour after this Montgomery left his headquarters and went first to see Horrocks, who told him of his dissatisfaction over 7th Motor Brigade. Montgomery suggested that Horrocks should take the brigade under his own direct command, and then went on to see Ramsden. While he was away on this trip Alexander arrived at 8th Army Headquarters. He had been delayed by dust storms and so missed seeing Montgomery. After a talk with de Guingand, he returned to Cairo.

This dust storm was at its height at one o'clock when the Afrika Korps set off again, now travelling north-east, and commanded by von Vaerst, the reconnaissance units pushing out on their right. This brought them up against 3rd County of London Yeomanry south of Ragil, and against 1st/60th round Samaket Gaballa, their route taking them directly across the eastern end of Ragil. This and the opposition from both Carr and Bosvile made progress slow. It was even slower in XX Corps on the left, in spite of the fact that the only opposition encountered was from the 10th Hussars. Littorio kept fairly well up close to the left flank of 21st Panzer, but Ariete in the middle and Trieste on the left were still tangled up in the minefields and could not start until three o'clock. By half past three Bosvile's columns were being pushed back by the reconnaissance units until they were six miles east of Ragil. At the same time 10th Hussars began to get anxious about their position. They saw themselves being cut off and asked for permission to withdraw. An argument then developed as to whether they should move east across the front of the enemy and rejoin Bosvile, or north to join Richards. Bosvile ordered them to do the former. Orders were later confirmed that they were to do the opposite; but by this time they were on the move and only just managed to cross the head of the advancing enemy, who forced them gradually north-eastwards until they came to rest up against the minefields of the Alam el Halfa position.

The whole area south of Bare Ridge was now a sea of dust and a fruitful source of rumour. Roberts' 22nd Armoured Brigade had stood to before first light in their positions round Point 102, west of Alam el Halfa. They had been on their toes ready for battle all through the hot and dusty day. Reports passed on from 7th Armoured Division did not give at all a clear picture of what was happening to the south and south-west of them. There was no doubt that there was a large number of enemy tanks somewhere about the eastern end of Ragil and to the north of it: but just how many and in what direction they were moving was difficult to tell. The brigade was grouped in a semi-circle facing south round two projecting small foothills, one south-east and one south-west of Point 102. Round the former and facing south-east was the regiment composed of 5th Royal Tank Regiment with two squadrons of 2nd Royal Gloucestershire Hussars. They had 23 Grants and 15 Crusader tanks. Just west of them, but round the corner of the foothill and facing south-west were 4th County of London Yeomanry with 22 Grants and 15 Crusaders. On the eastern side of the other foothill

and about a mile and a half west of the Yeomanry was the
anti-tank platoon of B Company, 1st Rifle Brigade, which
had four 6-pounders. To their west, facing almost due west,
was the regiment composed of 1st and 6th Royal Tanks. They
had 23 Grants and a light squadron of 19 Stuarts. North of
them, in the right rear of the position, was the anti-tank
battery. In reserve and hidden from view behind Point 102
were the Royal Scots Greys with 24 Grants and 21 Stuarts.
Roberts himself, with the 4 Crusader tanks of his headquarters, was on the south-east side of Point 102, the eighteen
25-pounders of 1st Royal Horse Artillery in position between him and 5th Royal Tanks. The whole position from
the 5th Royal Tanks on the eastern or left flank to the
1st/6th Royal tanks on the western or right flank was three
miles across. The Greys in reserve were about two miles
from the front of the position.

In the morning Roberts had ordered the light squadrons of
the County of London Yeomanry and of 5th Royal Tanks
(actually 'B' Squadron 4th County of London Yeomanry
and 'B' Squadron 2nd Gloucestershire Hussars) with Observation Post officers from 1st Royal Horse Artillery, to a
very slight ridge about three miles to the south. Now in the
afternoon, feeling the need of direct information of his own,
he told them to patrol further south and report on enemy
movement without getting involved. Some time later the
Yeomanry's Crusader squadron reported a strong force of
over 100 enemy tanks moving north-east to the south of
them. At half past five these light squadrons were in action
against the enemy, the Yeomanry losing one Crusader and
the Gloucestershire Hussars three before they withdrew.

At this time de Guingand spoke to Horrocks on the telephone to find out what was happening. He was told that about
100 German tanks had just been reported moving north-east
less than a mile south of Roberts; but nothing seemed to be
happening elsewhere, although there had been a report earlier
on of 60 tanks near Samaket Gaballa. While they were talk-
ing, a further report came in that the tanks south of Roberts
had turned east, leaving two 88-mm. guns facing the brigade.
Horrocks said that he expected a tank battle that evening.
Renton claimed that his division had knocked out 60 enemy

tanks, but Horrocks thought that 30 would be a more reasonable estimate. He had not taken over command of Bosvile as suggested.

After consulting with Freyberg, he had agreed that the latter would send out active company patrols that night with considerable artillery support and some tanks and anti-tank guns to penetrate to Munassib and then exploit south-west, returning at first light.

While this conversation was going on, 120 German tanks, mostly Mark IIIs but with some of the new Mark IV Specials in the lead, all believed to be of 21st Panzer Division, were approaching the telegraph line which ran obliquely across the front of Roberts' position, 1,000 yards from his forward tanks. They halted as they reached it and 30 tanks turned eastward. After a pause the rest moved north for a short way and then east. This meant that they were moving across the front of the County of London Yeomanry position, just out of effective range. It looked as if they had not realised that the brigade was there and would drive past it into 44th Division's position round Alam el Halfa. Roberts therefore told 5th Royal Tanks and the Yeomanry to show themselves and to be prepared to move out of their dug-in positions and take the enemy from the flank, if the latter continued to move east. As soon as they began to do this, just after six o'clock, the Germans woke up to their presence, halted, formed up rapidly into a fighting formation, turned north and made straight for 'A' Squadron of the Yeomanry. The dust was subsiding and visibility improving. There was only an hour's daylight left, and the light was in favour of our gunners, being slightly behind them and in the faces of the enemy. The German move brought them straight towards the slight re-entrant between the two foothills. Their right came directly against the northern Grant squadron of the Yeomanry, 'A' Squadron, while their left came straight towards 'B' Company of the 1st Rifle Brigade. When the leading tanks were less than 1000 yards from them, the Yeomanry opened up. The Germans halted and fired back, their guns being concentrated on 'A' Squadron. In a short time all 12 of their tanks were knocked out, but 'B' Squadron, who were slightly on the enemy's right flank, had been firing to good effect and the German tanks pulled back just out of range. Major Cameron, commanding 'A' Squadron, wrote afterwards:

We were under strict instructions not to open fire until so ordered, the hope being that the enemy would be deceived as to our true position until he had come in very close. However, well before the German tanks reached the telegraph poles, which we knew to be our maximum effective range, the Germans opened fire and already three tanks of my leading troop on the sugar-loaf were blazing before they had hardly fired a shot. In any event, the damage our guns could do at that range would have been negligible; but the Germans came on up to and even past the telegraph poles, by which time, of course, they were under intense fire from all along the line: I saw tank after tank going up in flames or being put out of action, and this including my own when the big gun became unserviceable. However, the German advance was momentarily checked and, although in the fog of battle it was difficult to know which of their tanks had been knocked out (German tanks seldom go on fire), the great thing was that they were not coming on in front. I ran over to the Commanding Officer's tank to say that I had lost touch by wireless with all my tanks, and attempted to present him with a picture of what was going on. He ordered me to report to the Brigadier some few hundred yards in the rear.

The destruction of Cameron's squadron had opened up a wide gap in the very centre of the position. Roberts did not want to move either of the flanking regiments into it, as there were still many more German tanks behind which could move round one or both of the flanks. The 30 which had originally turned east were now reported as 23 moving across the front of 5th Royal Tanks, out of range. While the artillery brought down heavy concentrations of fire on the Germans, Roberts ordered the Greys to move over the crest of Point 102 and down into the gap on the right of the Yeomanry. Soon after this the Germans began to advance again slowly, this time edging more to the west. The Rifle Brigade held their fire until the enemy were within 300 yards

and then opened up with their 6-pounders. Sergeant Griffiths
alone got five, and the platoon claimed 19 altogether. But
there was still no sign of the Greys. 'Come on the Greys,
get out your whips', said Roberts over the wireless to Fiennes,
their Colonel. Only half an hour's daylight left: the gap
still open, and nobody else to fill it. Checked for a time by
the Rifle Brigade, the German tanks came forward again.
The artillery thundered out, but this would not stop them.
Then came the Greys over the top. To Roberts and the
forward regiments it was 'at last'. To the Greys it had all
seemed a mad rush. Down the slope they thundered in clouds
of dust, Roberts by wireless directing them to fill the gap.
They went straight in as the light began to fade, and soon
their guns were hammering away. This put a stop to any
further enemy move in the centre. Interest now swung eastwards to the left flank. The tanks which had gone that way
had swung right round in face of the minefield in front of
133rd Brigade. Here 'B' Battery of 1st Royal Horse Artillery
took them on with armour-piercing shot over open sights. As
the Greys had now filled the gap in the centre, Roberts
moved the Yeomanry Crusaders round to plug this hole.

But by now the light had faded and the enemy drew off,
the main body turning south towards Ragil. The tanks on the
eastern flank drew back three miles to the east, but 6 of them
stayed close by all night. Roberts' losses had been low. The
County of London Yeomanry had lost 12 Grants and one
Crusader, with one man killed and 15 wounded; the Gloucestershire Hussars had lost 4 Crusaders, with 2 wounded;
the Greys 4 Grants; the Rifle Brigade's casualties were 2
killed and 30 wounded. The Brigade's tanks claimed to have
knocked out 22 enemy tanks; County of London Yeomanry
11, Greys 5, 5th Royal Tanks 6. The Rifle Brigade claimed
19, but some of these claims were duplicated, and the total
was thought to be about 30. 4th Light Armoured Brigade
claimed to have knocked out 35 to 40 tanks during the day,
and 7th Motor Brigade also claimed some. The total of all
claims came to 68; but in fact the total complete tank losses
of the Germans during the day seem to have been only 22,
although more than that had fallen out for one reason or
another. 21st Panzer had 72, and 15th Panzer 100 fit tanks

at the end of the day, the full establishment of each being 120.

This short sharp action round Point 102 in the last hour of daylight was the only significant event on the whole front in the second half of the day. The reconnaissance units and perhaps the right flank of 15th Panzer Division had pushed Carr off Samaket Gaballa. He was now back at Bir Mseilikh, 10 miles further east and about the same distance south-east of Custance's 8th Armoured Brigade, who had done nothing all day. 7th Motor Brigade was struggling back through soft sand to the area between them. In that hour's battle, on a front of only a few miles, in which certainly not more and probably less than 100 tanks on both sides had actually fired their guns against each other, the tide of battle in the desert had turned. It all seemed too easy, and does to this day. The explanations on neither side are wholly convincing. Even allowing for the delays of the night and morning, the progress of the Afrika Korps, the world's experts at 'blitzkrieg', was extraordinarily slow. They set off from the area south of Ragil at one o'clock by their time (two o'clock in 8th Army) and it took them three and a half hours to cover the 20 miles to Point 102. Rommel and Bayerlein make much play of the delay caused by the Italians being slow and not coming up on their left. It is true that they appear to have moved like snails against no opposition; but it was a new departure that the Afrika Korps should insist that they could not move unless their Italian brothers were closely in line, as if they were executing a wheel on the parade ground. No doubt the dust storm, thickened by the following wind, blowing their own dust round them, added to the delay caused by descending into Ragil and climbing out again. Slow work in soft sand, overheating from a following wind hot from the south, all no doubt increased their petrol consumption. If we are to believe the Germans it was this that caused them to call off the attack, although the gathering darkness must really have forced it on them. Whatever the true reason, there was no question of pushing on that night, and the Afrika Korps settled into leaguer, a few miles south of 22nd Armoured Brigade, with 21st Panzer Division on the left and the 15th on the right.

At this time Alexander and Montgomery were conferring together at the latter's headquarters. Earlier both had issued special orders of the day, Montgomery's using the words: 'No withdrawal and no surrender.' The only decision they took which is recorded is that 8th Armoured Division was to be moved from east of Cairo to west of the Nile, near the Pyramids. Montgomery arranged with Coningham for the Desert Air Force to lay on a heavy bombing attack on the area round Ragil, where concentrations of transport had been reported and it was thought that the Afrika Korps would spend the night: the landing grounds at Daba and Sidi Haneish, east of Mersa Matruh, were also to be attacked. 8th Army Intelligence were impressed with the difficulties that faced Rommel over transport. Montgomery gave orders accordingly that motor transport was to be the principal target of both the Air Force and the Army, and this there-fore figured prominently in the orders which Horrocks issued that evening to his divisional commanders. Freyberg and Hughes were to hold their present positions and take every opportunity for offensive action by artillery against enemy 'soft-skinned' vehicles. Renton was to continue to impose the maximum delay. Samaket Gaballa, which Horrocks does not seem to have realised was already in enemy hands, was to be held and only evacuated if attacked by superior forces. From it, attacks were to be launched against the enemy's 'maintenance and soft-skinned vehicles'. Gatehouse was to destroy the enemy attacking 13th Corps' battle positions and to prevent him establishing an anti-tank gun screen be-tween Custance and Roberts, or anywhere 'within field artil-lery range': finally Gatehouse was to manœuvre his brigades so as to prevent any part of his force being defeated in detail, with the proviso that Roberts' position round Point 102 was at no time to be left vacant. How these tasks were to be accomplished, and who was to decide the method by which they were to be done, remains a mystery. The decision that Custance was to join Roberts and Richards in the area be-tween Hughes and Freyberg was in fact taken by Montgomery

early the following morning, perhaps at the suggestion of
Horrocks. It was probably the latter, rather than Gatehouse,
who decided that the move should be made across the front
of Hughes' position and not round the back of Alam el Halfa.

For 8th Army it was generally a quiet night. Hughes'
artillery poured masses of shells into the area three miles
east of Roberts and just south of Lee's 133rd brigade, where
rumour had it that 15th Panzer Division were forming up for
a night attack, which was in fact far from their intention.
Wellingtons and Albacores carried out heavy and repeated
attacks near the eastern end of Ragil. The bombs fell mostly
on the Reconnaissance Group, which suffered heavy casualties as a result. Little of the petrol which Cavallero had promised to Rommel had yet arrived. Rommel, in his memoirs,
says that in addition his supply traffic through the lanes in
the minefields were being seriously disturbed by British
armour 'south of the salient'; but this cannot have been so
until a considerably later stage in the battle. There had
been no British forces of any kind anywhere near the minefields since the morning, nor were there to be again for a
day or two. Rommel states, however, that it was his supply
difficulties which forced him to give up any attempt at
major action and to avoid all large-scale movement of his
motorised forces. Accordingly operations next day were to
be limited to an attack by 15th Panzer Division only, which
was apparently to try and capture Alam el Halfa all on its
own.

Of all Rommel's decisions this seems one of the most
curious. It can only be explained if one assumes that he
thought that Roberts' position marked the extreme eastern
edge of 8th Army's defences, and that Alam el Halfa itself
was not properly held. It also assumes his ignorance of the
position of Custance. The pilots of the Stukas which had
attacked Alam el Halfa during the day should have been
able to enlighten him on all these points. The impression
one gets is that he knew he could not pursue his original
plan, but could not steel himself to abandon it altogether
or just do nothing. He therefore ordered a half-hearted
compromise solution which could not do any harm and

might even result in some unexpected and surprising success.

When Montgomery considered the position on the morning of September 1st, he appreciated that there was no longer any great danger of a bold outflanking move east of Alam el Halfa and decided, as has been told, to concentrate all three armoured brigades under Gatehouse, a total of about 500 tanks, between Freyberg and Hughes. The plan which he arrived at by mid-day, and communicated to his corps commanders when he visited them in the afternoon, was that Ramsden should thin out and begin to form a reserve and that Horrocks should gradually close the gap between the New Zealanders and Himeimat, while Renton's armoured cars were to work round Rommel's southern flank and 'tap in', as he put it, at Himeimat. Lumsden's 10th Corps, the headquarters of which was to be established that day at El Imayid, on the coast 15 miles east of El Alamein, was to be prepared to command all the reserve available and push through to Daba. Morshead's 9th Australian Division was 'possibly' to pass to his command. At this stage therefore Montgomery saw himself cutting off Rommel and putting all the forces which had taken part in the attack 'in the bag': thereafter exploiting his victory westwards. When he reached Horrocks at Alam el Halfa that afternoon, his arrival coinciding with a severe Stuka attack, he was to be given news of the morning's operations which must have made him less optimistic.

Soon after first light 15th Panzer Division had tried again to work round Roberts' left flank, as they had the evening before. They were engaged by his tanks, but soon gave up their attempt in order to meet the threat which was developing on their right flank from Custance. For two of this brigade's regiments, the Nottinghamshire Yeomanry or Sherwood Rangers, and the Staffordshire Yeomanry, it was their first action since being converted from horses; but the other, 3rd Royal Tank Regiment, was a veteran. Gatehouse told Custance, who was in his first desert battle, to move on a broad front south of the minefield in front of Hughes to a position just east of Roberts. On arrival he was 'to be pre-

pared to operate against the enemy's right flank'. In ampli-
fication of this Gatehouse added that, as the brigade might
be needed later to counter-attack the enemy's northern flank
if he attempted a wider move round Alam el Halfa, Custance
was not to get too deeply involved or to accept needless
casualties.

The brigade started off at half past six. Two hours later
3rd Royal Tanks in the lead had covered about eight miles
when they met 28 enemy tanks. The Staffordshire Yeomanry
came up on their left and, after a short exchange of shots
and a few casualties, both regiments withdrew from contact. The Sherwood Rangers were then told to try further to
the right, which brought them up to the minefields in front
of Hughes. With these on their right they pushed forward
until, at a range of 800 yards, they came under heavy fire
from the enemy and lost 7 tanks. At this, faithful to his
instructions, Custance gave up further attempts to press
forward for the time being. This had drawn the Germans off
Roberts, who thereafter spent an entirely peaceful day. On
Richards' front there had been signs of the enemy forming
up to launch an attack, which was the signal for an immense
outburst of artillery fire, one battery alone firing 2,000 rounds.
There is no record of the enemy having in fact intended to
attack, and he was certainly not encouraged to do so after
this.

Further south Bosvile had gingerly re-established contact
with the German Reconnaissance Group, roughly on a line
running due south from Alam el Halfa. Carr was engaged in
regrouping his brigade into three columns of tanks, motor
infantry and guns to operate against von Vaerst's southern
flank. However, during the day they did not succeed in
getting beyond the armoured car screen which was still east
of Samaket Gaballa.

The situation that Horrocks had to describe first to Alexander in the morning, and later to Montgomery in the afternoon, was not therefore one that held out great hopes of
exploitation by Lumsden.

While Montgomery was with Horrocks, Custance was
again trying to advance, after a concentration of all the artillery which the Corps could bring to bear had bombarded

15th Panzer Division in front of him. The Germans withdrew a mile or two to the south, according to them because of petrol shortage, and the brigade arrived in a position just east of Roberts by a quarter past three. It was an uncomfortable situation. They were on a forward slope with no suitable hull-down positions, and with minefields immediately behind them and to their left rear. If the Germans attacked, it would be a very different affair from the carefully chosen positions of Roberts on their right.

However they were in fact in no danger from such an attack. Following on the night attacks, the Royal Air Force had flown 122 light bomber sorties during the day, mostly against targets in and around Ragil. In von Vaerst's headquarters alone seven officers were killed, and Rommel himself, who drove up to the front in the middle of the day, had a narrow escape when an 8-inch bomb splinter went straight through a spade by the side of the slit trench in which he was taking refuge. A red-hot fragment of metal actually fell beside him. The air attacks, the ability of the artillery to fire vast quantities of ammunition apparently almost endlessly, his casualties in men, but particularly in vehicles, and his precarious petrol position, all caused him during the afternoon to consider seriously abandoning the whole operation. However he deferred a final decision and sent a laconic and uninformative report to OKW that night merely reporting the failure of Morshead's raid on Tel el Eisa, the arrival of a convoy at Suez, and the heavy air attacks to which he was subjected. He still had not lost many tanks, the total number of fit tanks of the two German Panzer divisions being about 150, not more than 13 at the most having been knocked out that day. Custance had lost 3 Crusaders and 13 Grants, 3 men being killed and 26 wounded. The brigade's total of fit tanks had dropped to 60, largely because of breakdowns, while Roberts still had 152 and Richards 100. Carr had 52 light tanks at the end of the day.

The Wellingtons and Albacores returned to their attacks around Ragil after dark. They went on all night, and by dawn on September 2nd, Rommel and everybody else having had enough, he made the final decision to abandon the offensive. It no longer had any hope of success, partly because of

E.A.   C the petrol situation and the air attacks, partly because from now on it could only develop into a slogging match in which material strength, which was all in Montgomery's favour, would decide the issue. He decided then to go right back to where he had started, to the area of Qaret el Abd and Gebel Kalakh, and to begin thinning out that day.

On neither side did it prove to be an active day, except in the air, the Royal Air Force flying 167 bomber and 501 fighter sorties over the area. In the evening Horrocks warned Freyberg that he would have to attack to start closing the gap on the night of the following day, September 3rd. 5th Indian Brigade would relieve 132nd Brigade of 44th Division, which would then become available to him for the attack. In the morning one of Carr's columns, commanded by and largely composed of 4th/8th Hussars, scored a signal success when it surprised 300 lorries five miles east of Himeimat and destroyed 57 of them, pursuing the remainder north as far as the ridge between Himeimat and Samaket Gaballa. At the same time patrols of 11th Hussars had worked round to the south-west of Himeimat. This good news reached Montgomery about the time that he was giving orders personally to Lumsden 'to prepare to take command of all reserves available and push through to Daba'. He followed his usual routine of leaving his headquarters in time to reach Horrocks at half past two, calling in to see Ramsden on his way back.

It was after these visits that he came to the conclusion that, although the Panzer Armee was almost encircled, he would not rush in to attack it, and told Horrocks to 'shoot up, harry and destroy the enemy's motor transport' and 'gradually and methodically close the gap'. Montgomery appreciated that Rommel had now finally abandoned his offensive and his plan was that on the night of September 3rd Freyberg was to extend his area southwards to a depth of three miles. Next day he would be reinforced by 151st Brigade, all that was left of 50th Division, which could then free one of the New Zealand brigades to resume the attack two nights later to bring them down to Munassib by the morning of September 6th, four days ahead. They would still then be six miles from Himeimat.

Towards the end of the day there were some signs of enemy withdrawal towards Ragil, but an attempt by 4th/8th Hussars to attack motor transport two miles east of Himeimat was held off by 25 enemy tanks and by anti-tank guns on the line of the escarpment. These were a group from Ariete sent there after the morning's attack. The enemy was getting sensitive to 'tapping in' at Himeimat.

That evening Kesselring came to see Rommel, who gave him a first-hand account of the damage being inflicted by the British light bomber squadrons with their strong fighter escorts. The Germans had christened them 'Party Rally' squadrons, their impeccable formation of 18 aircraft resembling the displays given by the Luftwaffe at the annual Nazi Party Rally at Nuremburg. Kesselring promised to do all he could and to reinforce Egypt with fighters.

After their talk Rommel sent a long signal to OKW to justify his decision to abandon the offensive. He began by saying that the failure to supply him with petrol was the main reason why he could not continue. He gave a detailed statement of the position, which showed that he could only continue at the full rate of expenditure until September 5th. In the last two days only 2,610 tons of petrol had arrived, 3,352 tons, the equivalent of five and a half daily issues, having been sunk. Half of the petrol which Cavallero had promised would arrive by September 3rd had already been sunk. If the two tankers due at Tobruk next day, the *Bianchi* and the *Sportivo*, succeeded in unloading their full cargoes, he would still only have enough to last until September 7th. Diesel stocks for the Italian lorries were even lower and the ammunition position was little better.

Rommel went on to give two other reasons for breaking off his attack. The first was the loss of surprise due to the fact that the area of his attack had not, as had been thought, been only weakly occupied and partially mined; but contained several deep minefields, kilometres thick, and many obstacles, the presence of both being previously unsuspected. Finally the heavy air attacks, continuing day and night without pause, had caused considerable losses in men and material and were seriously affecting the morale of both Germans and Italians, as well as rendering the supply situation even more precar-

ious. He finished up by saying: 'The Army, therefore, will
fall back slowly under enemy pressure to the starting line,
unless the supply and the air situation are fundamentally
changed.'

No sooner had the message been signed than the nightly
air attacks resumed with redoubled fury. Seventy-two Wellingtons and Albacores attacked Ragil, dropping among other
things two 4,000-pound bombs to the accompaniment of
flares, which lit up the whole area and could not be extin-
guished. Apart from this the night was quiet, and neither
the New Zealand Division nor the 44th had any contact
with the enemy. By the morning of September 3rd, the
layout of Rommel's forces from left to right was as follows.
Opposite the south-west corner of the New Zealand Division's
position, the Bersaglieri of Brescia had been strengthened
by Ramcke's Parachute Brigade. To their right 90th Light
Division extended the line eastwards to Muhafid, part of
the division being in reserve to the west. XX Corps had
Trieste on the left and Littorio on the right in Muhafid and
the depression to the east of it south of 23rd Armoured
Brigade. Ariete was south of Muhafid between the other
divisions and Ragil. The Afrika Korps had 21st Panzer
Division round the south-east corner of the depression east of
Muhafid and 15th Panzer Division extending south to the
eastern end of Ragil. The Reconnaissance Group took on from
there all the way to Himeimat, which was held by a battalion
from Folgore. They were backed up by a group of 25 tanks
from Ariete. The picture of the enemy available to 8th Army
was more or less accurate, except that they thought 90th
Division was in process of relief by Triestes. First light
reports said that the enemy had withdrawn slightly to the
west and that fires and derelict vehicles could be seen in
Ragil.

It was Sunday and a national day of prayer. Before
Montgomery went to church at eight, he gave orders that
there was to be no forward movement from the main battle
positions except by patrols, which were to concentrate on
the destruction of the enemy's motor transport. Horrocks
was to proceed vigorously with the plan for closing the gap,
working carefully and methodically southwards from the New

Zealand positions to Himeimat.

It was a quiet morning for the Army and all who could attended church services. The Air Force however were busy and at mid-day reported signs of enemy withdrawal: 1,000 vehicles were seen to be moving west to the north of Ragil. An hour and a half later they said that the enemy were withdrawing in three columns on the routes of their original advance. This caused considerable excitement at Army, who told Horrocks to get Renton to operate vigorously northwards from the escarpment between Samaket Gaballa and Himeimat. They also called for renewed air attacks.

Horrocks spoke to the GSO1 of 7th Armoured Division, Renton being away from his headquarters at the time. He ordered the division to attack the southern flank with both Carr's and Bosvile's brigades. He was told that 4th/8th Hussars had already found the enemy stronger in this area and had been unable to get back to the position on the escarpment from which they had operated successfully the day before. Attempts to move further south had led to guns and wheeled vehicles getting stuck in the soft sand. It was not therefore possible for Bosvile, who was engaging the enemy at the east end of Ragil, to operate round that flank, apart from the time it would take to get his troops there. Carr's operations were liable to be restricted to his light tanks, without artillery or anti-tank gun support.

When Renton returned to his headquarters, he confirmed this and ordered Carr to operate as offensively as he could south of the escarpment, while Bosvile did the same in a westerly direction north of it. Next day 7th Motor Brigade was to enter Ragil and report by half past six in the morning if it were occupied by the enemy or not, while Carr was to report by seven o'clock if the enemy was still on his side of the eastern minefield north of the escarpment. As soon as possible after first light one regiment of light tanks was to attack as far north as possible west of this minefield. Armoured cars were to patrol as far north as they could to harass and cut off the enemy.

While these plans for 7th Armoured Division had been discussed, New Zealand Division were preparing for Operation

'Beresford' that night. Their task was to attack due south from their positions on Bare Ridge between the first and the fourth minefields to a depth of 6,000 yards on a frontage of 5,000, thus capturing the enemy positions on the northern edge of Munassib.

Robertson's 132nd Brigade of 44th Division, already under Freyberg's command, was to attack on the west, and Kippenberger's 5th New Zealand Brigade on the east.

Robertson had a hectic day preparing and had to adjust his plan to meet Freyberg's insistence that his tanks, Valentines of 46th Royal Tanks, should not lead and that the attack should be 'silent', that is without artillery support. Owing to chaotic confusion in the assembly area zero hour had to be postponed several times. When the attack did eventually start after midnight, it was far from silent and was illuminated by a burning truck. Neither 5th Royal West Kents on the right nor the 4th on the left could make headway against the defences on the northern lip of the Munassib, all communication broke down, Robertson himself was wounded and his brigade major eventually managed to re-organise the brigade 1,000 yards short of their objectives.

On the left Kippenberger's 5th Brigade had been rather more successful, but in a fit of over-enthusiasm the Maoris on the right had veered away to the west while 21st Battalion on the left had diverged eastwards, leaving a wide gap in the centre. The Valentines of 50th Royal Tanks, mistaking German Very lights for lamps to mark a lane forward, went too far into this gap and lost 12 tanks, mostly on mines, Hughes their squadron commander being killed.

By first light on September 4th therefore the attack had gained less than two miles of largely unoccupied desert, the front line now being on an exposed forward slope, at a cost of 700 casualties in 132nd Brigade and 124 in 5th New Zealand. 6th New Zealand, carrying out a diversionary attack on Robertson's right flank, had lost 159, their Brigadier, George Clifton, being among those captured. The attack seems to have made very little impression on the enemy, Rommel dismissing it in the few words: 'A night attack on X Italian Corps cost the British particularly heavy losses, including many dead and 200 prisoners.' Certainly

Kippenberger's claim to have killed 500 of the enemy could not be substantiated. Rommel goes on to describe his interview with that irrepressible character George Clifton, who escaped that evening from a lavatory, only to be picked up a few days later by some German staff officers who were hunting gazelle.

During the day, Rommel continued to withdraw, maintaining the same general layout of his forces and delivering several counter-attacks against Freyberg's new positions. His nightly report to OKW spoke of the successful repulse of several attacks and as usual drew attention to his petrol situation. A ship with 800 tons had docked that day, but his situation was still critical and reserves would only last for another week.

Alexander arrived that evening for a talk with Montgomery, who had already decided not to persevere with the plan to 'close the gap'. Orders were given for Freyberg to withdraw to his original line. If the enemy themselves withdrew, he was to stay where he was, while Gatehouse and Renton were to follow up with patrols and 'light armoured formations', the armoured brigades of the former remaining in the existing positions west of Alam el Halfa. Renton's pressure on Rommel's right flank had not been very effective and little attempt seems to have been made by Carr to carry out the orders of the previous evening. The constant movement in the soft sand had reduced his tank strength to only 8 Crusaders in the Sharpshooters and 15 Stuarts in 4th/8th Hussars, who had spent the day in a fruitless manœuvre well to the south of Samaket Gaballa.

During the night, while Wellingtons and Albacores claimed great successes against transport packed tight in Ragil, the New Zealand division withdrew to its original line, Freyberg issuing an order of the day which claimed that 'when our losses are compared with those of the enemy and when we consider the effect that it had on enemy plans, the operation cannot be regarded as anything but an outstanding success'. The reference to its effect on the enemy was based on an opinion, said to have been expressed by Montgomery, that it was this action which forced Rommel to make a quick decision to withdraw and abandon for the present his intention to advance into Egypt. We know now that he had made this decision thirty-six hours earlier.

At dawn on September 5th the enemy was found to have withdrawn another few miles to just west of the old fourth or eastern minefield, thence westward to Himeimat. Cloud hampered the RAF from finding out more. Rommel's evening report announced his intention not to go right back to his original position, but to stop on the line of the British minefields with the Afrika Korps in reserve behind, two battle groups only being sent north to back up XXI Corps.

Although Montgomery had abandoned the attempt to 'close the gap' from the north, he still thought that Rommel would withdraw further and throughout the Army there was a general feeling of relaxation. Renton's patrols had in the morning reported the enemy to be moving west of the first and second minefields, covered by a strong rearguard of 70 tanks and many anti-tank guns, and about 1,000 vehicles had been seen by the RAF between Himeimat and Kalakh. By last light Bosvile's riflemen were in the area of Ragil and 4th/8th Hussars, who had tried to get round the southern flank, had been stopped by enemy tanks three miles east of Himeimat. During the day an armoured car patrol of 11th Hussars had again made its way along the northern edge of the Qattara depression to the foot of the pass at Naqb abu Dweis, which it found still occupied. These activities were given an optimistic tinge in the order of the day which Montgomery issued that evening. 'The Battle of Alamein', he said, 'has now lasted for six days and the enemy has slowly and surely been driven from 8th Army's area. Tonight, September 5th, his rearguards are being driven through the minefield area north of Himeimat.' He went on to congratulate everyone on the heavy defeat of the enemy which would have far-reaching results.

His orders that evening told Horrocks to re-establish his original positions and to dominate the area as far west as Gebel Kalakh and El Taqa, the task of doing this being passed on to Renton.

It was a quiet night with no bombing and Rommel's forces withdrew unmolested almost to their final positions. 15th Panzer Division went all the way back to near Kalakh, while the 21st stopped just west of the minefields, leaving a Panzer Grenadier battalion and an anti-tank battalion with a company of tanks and a battery of guns still east of the second minefield.

The battle was now over and both Rommel and Montgomery realised it. The former sent a long report the following night to OKW in which he emphasised the weight of the British artillery fire, but pointed out that he had always succeeded in fending off attacks by tanks and reconnaissance units. He claimed that during the battle his forces had destroyed 124 tanks and armoured reconnaissance vehicles, a claim which could only be justified by including Bren-gun carriers, which it must have done. He also claimed 1,000 other vehicles, 10 guns, 22 anti-tank guns, and 400 prisoners. He gave the German losses as 369 killed, 1,163 wounded, and 272 missing, and the Italian as 167 killed, 587 wounded, and 297 missing. They had lost 36 German and 11 Italian tanks and armoured reconnaissance vehicles, 277 German and 97 Italian other vehicles, 11 German and 6 Italian guns, 20 German and 16 Italian anti-tank guns. These figures did not include vehicles damaged and recovered, which in the case of German tanks amounted to 76.

Rommel stated that most of the losses were due to continued air attack and the very high expenditure of ammunition by the British artillery. On the now monotonous theme of his supply situation he said his petrol would last for eight days at the rate he had been using it. Fourteen days of battle would bring his ammunition down to his final reserve, and he had enough food and other supplies for twenty-three days. Finally he asked for the German 22nd Infantry Division to be sent over from Greece with vehicles and the necessary supply troops.

Montgomery had now realised that Rommel was not going to withdraw any more, and at seven o'clock in the morning of the 7th, he finally decided to call off all further attempts to push him further back, 'influenced', he said, 'by the definite advantage in keeping the enemy down in the south'.

By the end of the battle 8th Army's tank strength had altered little. On August 31st, of its total of 945, 772 were

with units in the forward area, and 695 of those fit for action:
197 Crusaders, 169 Stuarts, 164 Grants and 163 Valentines.
On September 8th these totals had fallen respectively to
896, 674 and 598: the Army also had nearly 400 armoured
cars.

Freyberg attributed the enemy's failure, in a situation in
which they could not find room for manœuvre, to their in-
ability to carry out a proper infantry attack in co-operation
with artillery. He accused them of having become tank
followers. Montgomery drew many lessons from the battle,
which he distributed in a note on September 7th. He emphasised the need for a sound initial framework and a firm
control from Army Headquarters. He stressed the importance
of having a strong well-built defence and of forcing the
enemy to attack it. His main point, which he was constantly
to re-emphasise, was that one should not be deflected from
one's plan by the enemy's moves: 'no dancing to the enemy's
tune'.

Rommel attributed his defeat to the great superiority of
his opponents in the air, and their lavish availability of
artillery ammunition, his own shortage of supplies, particularly petrol, and the fatal delay on the first night due to the
unsuspected intricacy and depth of the British minefields.

In sum Montgomery's victory was founded on the fact
that he had enough forces, backed by ample fire-power, to
ensure a fully adequate defence on a front which his opponent could not outflank: an enviable position, but one which,
in the short time he had been there, he had made vigorous
efforts to bring about.

As soon as he realised that the Battle of Alam el Halfa was really over, Montgomery lost no time in applying himself and everyone else to preparations for the decisive blow which was later to be known as the Battle of El Alamein. His immediate policy rested on three bases. First security: the positions already held must be firmly secured as the start line. Secondly training: the experiences of Alam el Halfa had strengthened his belief that all arms needed as much training as it was possible to give them. Finally, and very much linked with training, he had to reshuffle units in order that they should be organised as soon as possible into the formations and under the commanders chosen for the battle itself.

To meet the first need, three new minefields were laid in the south to take the place of those now occupied by the enemy. They were called Nuts, May and June. Nuts linked up the middle of the old fourth minefield in Muhafid with the northern end of the old third minefield south of Ragil, and was finished by September 11th. May was three miles east of this and ran south from Bare Ridge through the eastern end of Ragil to Samaket Gaballa, beyond which it ran south-east for five miles. June was laid between the two, from the south edge of Ragil to three miles south-west of Samaket Gaballa.

To meet the needs of training and reorganisation, it was of particular importance to get on quickly with the preparation for battle of 10th Corps. Lumsden, former Commander of 1st Armoured Division, had been appointed to command this corps at the time of Montgomery's arrival. The latter wanted to have a man of his own, not one of the old desert hands and a cavalier to boot. However Alexander was not prepared to make a clean sweep of all the old commanders, particularly not one with a fighting reputation like Lumsden's, and the influence of his Chief of Staff, McCreery, a fellow

12th Lancer, was strongly behind this. Montgomery reluctantly gave way. The Corps Headquarters had been brought hurriedly up from the Delta on September 1st in the hope of commanding the pursuit. The first step was for it to exchange signals with 30th Corps, whose signals were equipped and trained for mobile warfare. It then moved to the area of the Wadi Natrun to start training with the formations it was to command. They were to be 1st, 8th and 10th Armoured Divisions and the New Zealand Division, reorganised with two of its own brigades, 5th and 6th, and 9th Armoured Brigade. The latter had formed part of 1st Cavalry Division in Palestine, recently converted to 10th Armoured Division, and consisted of 3rd Hussars, the Royal Wiltshire and the Warwickshire Yeomanry.

The first step in reorganising was for Headquarters 4th Indian Division to relieve Headquarters 5th Indian Division in the line, 7th Indian Brigade relieving 9th Indian Brigade at the same time: the rest of the division, 5th and 161st Indian Brigades, the artillery and the divisional troops remained unchanged. The next was to bring up Wimberley's 51st Highland Division and get it together again. The division had reached Egypt from England in August and stayed round Cairo. During the battle of Alam el Halfa two of its brigades had been sent up to 8th Army, but had taken no active part in the battle. On September 9th Wimberley brought the rest of the division up from Cairo, and on the 10th they relieved 44th Division in the Alam el Halfa position, operationally under 13th Corps, but under 30th Corps for training.

Hughes' 44th Division moved west to relieve the New Zealanders in their Bare Ridge position, losing Lee's 133rd Brigade which went to join 10th Corps as a lorried infantry brigade, but taking under its wing Percy's 151st Brigade, all that was left of the 50th Division, and also the 1st Greek Independent Brigade, newly arrived from the Delta where it had been formed of refugees from Greece.

On relief, the New Zealand Division moved to a seaside rest area near Burg el Arab for a week, before joining 10th Corps in its training area north-west of Wadi Natrun, taking Currie's 9th Armoured Brigade under its command.

7th Armoured Division was the next to be affected. It was to lose to 1st Armoured Division Bosvile's 7th Motor Brigade, which included one of its original motor battalions, 2nd Rifle Brigade. Renton himself had commanded this battalion in the early years and then the Motor Brigade itself. The substitution of the rhinoceros sign of 1st Armoured Division for the 7th's jerboa or desert rat was a change that did not come easily to many, and some curious hybrid animals were seen painted on vehicle mudguards for a long time after. Renton himself was also to go. There had been several differences of opinion between him and Horrocks before and during Alam el Halfa, and Montgomery wanted new blood here too. The choice, an ideal one, fell on John Harding, still Deputy Chief of Staff in Cairo. In return Roberts' 22nd Armoured Brigade came back to the division, and a month later the southern sector, held by 4th Light Armoured Brigade, was taken over by General Koenig's 1st Free French Brigade, also under the division's command. 7th Motor Brigade had a rest by the sea for a week before moving to Khatatba in the last week of September to join Briggs' 1st Armoured Division on its arrival there from the Delta, where it had been re-equipping since the beginning of August.

With the move of 10th Armoured Division and its 8th Armoured Brigade in the middle of September to a training area west of the Wadi Natrun, 10th Corps was complete, 8th Armoured Division also from the Delta, with Kenchington's 24th Armoured Brigade having moved up south-east of Wadi Natrun earlier in the month. The unsolved problem, however, was the provision of motor or 'lorried infantry' brigades for all these armoured divisions. The 7th, as we have seen, was left without one, its own having gone to the 1st. Lee's 133rd Brigade was removed from 44th Division, its infantry battalions hastily converted and reorganised, and was sent first to join 8th Armoured Division, and then, at the end of September, to the 10th. It was found impossible to produce another lorried infantry brigade to complete the 8th Division. Kenchington's brigade therefore joined the 10th as an extra brigade, the divisional troops under the Commander Royal Artillery, Brigadier 'Hammer' Mathew, were

formed into 'Hammerforce' in 10th Corps reserve, and the
divisional headquarters and signals to the disappointment of
its commander, Gairdner, were used for deception purposes
to take the place of Headquarters 10th Corps, when the
latter moved forward.

It was not therefore until nearly the end of September
that 10th Corps was fully assembled round the Wadi Natrun,
100 miles behind the front.

30th Corps' problems were simpler. The change over from
5th to 4th Indian Division and the arrival of the Highland
Division has been described. 9th Australian and 1st South
African Divisions were already in the Corps and holding the
line. The principal change was the arrival of a new Commander, Lieutenant-General Oliver Leese. He too was a
Montgomery man, like Horrocks, although a very different
type. In contrast to the intense, flamboyant and mercurial
impression created by Horrocks, he seemed a giant of solid
strength and forceful good humour. Forty-eight years old, he
had won a DSO at the age of twenty with the Coldstream
Guards in France in 1916. After a sound career between
the wars, in which he had been Brigade Major of the 1st
Guards Brigade, commanded the 1st Battalion, and been
Regimental Colonel of the Coldstream, he had been pro-
moted from a brigadier on the staff in France in 1940 to
command three divisions in succession, the West Sussex,
15th Scottish and Guards Armoured. On September 13th he
replaced Ramsden, whose old division, the 50th Northumbrian, was the only other one involved. In the middle of
the Battle of Alam el Halfa the division had been told to
produce a composite brigade, the 151st, from all its units
and was threatened with disbandment. Next day Nichols
heard that 2,000 reinforcements had arrived at the infantry
base depot in the Delta for his regiments. He begged to be
allowed to preserve the division and won his appeal. 69th
Brigade was reformed and, on October 5th, the division
took over the old New Zealand positions from 44th Division,
having the Greeks as its third brigade.

Concurrently with this great reshuffle, greatly complicating and being complicated by it, an intense programme of re-equipment was in train. The most important item was tanks, and in this respect the arrival of the 300 American Shermans on September 3rd was the most significant. In the five and a half weeks from the end of Alam el Halfa to the opening of the battle of El Alamein, 8th Army's tank strength rose from 896 to 1,351, made up of 285 Shermans, 246 Grants, 421 Crusaders, 167 Stuarts, 223 Valentines, 6 Matildas and 3 Churchills. Of these, 1,136 were with units in the forward area and 1,021 fit for action on the evening of October 23rd. The regiments of 8th and 9th Armoured Brigades each had a squadron of Shermans, one of Grants and one of Crusaders, while in 2nd and 24th Brigades the Grants were replaced by Shermans. 23rd Armoured Brigade was all Valentines. 22nd Armoured Brigade's regiments had two heavy squadrons each of Grants, their light squadrons being Crusaders, except for 1st Royal Tank Regiment which had Stuarts. The Greys in 4th Light Armoured Brigade had one squadron of Grants and two of Stuarts, while 4th/8th Hussars continued to have Stuarts only, as did the New Zealand Divisional Cavalry. 9th Australian Divisional Cavalry had both Stuarts and Crusaders. The troop of three Churchills on trial was with 7th Motor Brigade.

There was significant improvement in the Army's anti-tank armoury: 2-pounder guns increased in number from 450 to 550, and 6-pounders from 400 to 850. This made it possible to give each infantry battalion eight 2-pounders, and each motor battalion sixteen 6-pounders. The gunner anti-tank regiments had 6-pounders throughout, except for one battery in each infantry division. Medium artillery was doubled to a strength of 52 guns, and field artillery increased by 216 guns to a total of 832.

The Desert Air Force was also increased, until it had two mobile fighter groups and two light bomber wings available. Coningham's immediate policy was to rest, reorganise and train his squadrons. He therefore reduced fighter and light bomber operations and withdrew most of them to base airfields in the Delta. Heavy and medium bomber operations were however maintained against the enemy's ports. Between September 6th and October 22nd the Royal Air Force carried out 183 heavy and 903 medium bomber sorties, and the United States Air Force 120 sorties. The former concentrated on Tobruk, which was attacked by an average of 20 to 30 Wellingtons every night, while the longer range American Liberators went for Benghazi, their heaviest and most successful raid being on the night of September 22nd.

While these intricate problems were absorbing the attention and effort of 8th Army, the Commanders-in-Chief Middle East decided to carry out a series of diversionary operations to occupy the attention of the enemy. The principal one was to be a seaborne raid on Tobruk, accompanied by smaller raids from the landward elsewhere in Cyrenaica. The seeds of this operation had been sown much earlier, at the time when Auchinleck was battling for Ruweisat Ridge, when the Admiralty thought the situation so serious that they suggested sending a destroyer, which they were prepared to lose, to bombard Tobruk at dawn after the arrival there of an enemy convoy. Admiral Sir Henry Harwood, Commander-in-Chief Mediterranean, wished to expand this into a sea landing to cut Rommel's supply line and prevailed upon his fellow Commanders-in-Chief to support the operation in spite of the reiterated advice of their Joint Planning Staff that it would be fruitless and expensive.

The night of September 13th was selected for the operation, which was to consist of simultaneous raids on Tobruk and Benghazi with diversionary attacks on Barce and Gialo. It was thought that there was a brigade of low-grade Italian troops in Tobruk and that the only Germans were about 1,000 administrative troops some 15 miles to the east. The main force for the attack on Tobruk was known as Force A and consisted of 11th Royal Marine Commando (Lieutenant-Colonel Unwin) with detachments of heavy anti-aircraft artillery to man and dismantle captured guns, and engineers for demolition. It totalled little more than 400 men and was to be landed north of the harbour from two destroyers, HMS *Sikh* and HMS *Zulu*. At the same time a small inlet east of the harbour entrance was to be captured by Force B, 40 men of the 1st Special Air Service Regiment. They were to be accompanied by a large number of small detachments designed to man or destroy captured equipment, bringing the total including drivers to 80. This party was to be reinforced on its objective by Force C, 100 men of 1st Argyll and Sutherland Highlanders with detachments of other units adding another 100, transported all the way from Alexandria in 18 motor torpedo-boats and motor launches of the Royal Navy.

After a heavy bombardment of the harbour by the RAF, these three forces were to capture and hold the harbour for twenty-four hours while they caused as much damage as possible to shipping and the port. The whole force was then to be withdrawn by sea or, if enough enemy transport had been captured and the situation justified it, to continue raiding and then retire by land to Kufra. This ambitious and complicated operation was to be accompanied by raids by the Long Range Desert Group and the Special Air Service Regiment on Benghazi and Barce and the capture of Gialo as an intermediate base between Kufra and the various objectives.

The approach to Tobruk went according to plan and the most difficult and daring part of it, the capture of the coast defence and anti-aircraft guns on the south side of the eastern end of the harbour, was successfully carried out by Force B who then gave the success signal. This was a remarkable achievement after a journey totalling 1,700 miles since they left Cairo on August 22nd. The reinforcement of this party by Force C was however a total failure, the force eventually returning to Alexandria, having landed only ten men of the Royal Northumberland Fusiliers and lost five craft.

HM Ships *Sikh* and *Zulu* had arrived two miles off the northern arm of Tobruk harbour soon after three in the morning, but the landing was interfered with by a heavy swell with the result that only 150 men were ashore at four o'clock, two miles west of the point planned. By this time the enemy, who were considerably stronger than had been estimated, were thoroughly alert and had little difficulty in rounding up the Marines, who had got split up into small parties and soon ran out of ammunition. The destroyers fared no better. HMS *Sikh* was hit by gunfire from the shore and taken in tow by HMS *Zulu*, but had to be scuttled when the tow-rope was severed by a lucky enemy shell.

Force B now realised that Force A's landing must have failed and, after some severe fighting, Lieutenant-Colonel Haselden ordered those he was still in touch with to withdraw as best they could, he himself being killed in the attempt.

HMS *Zulu* had survived three air attacks on her way back when she came in sight of the destroyer HMS *Coventry*, on fire as a result of air attack and abandoned. She sank her with two torpedoes, but was then herself hit in the engine-room by the last bomb of a further attack. She was taken in tow but sank at eight o'clock that night, the survivors being transferred to two other destroyers. They arrived at Alexandria in the morning of September 15th, the soldiers at least excessively thankful to reach dry land again.

The total losses, including the crew of HMS *Sikh* who were captured, came to 700 of whom probably about 100 were killed, while the Germans and Italians suffered 180 casualties, a large number of Italians being killed. It was an expensive failure and the possibility of success had never been high, as the Joint Planning Staff had pointed out.

The raid on Benghazi under Lieutenant-Colonel David Stirling had failed to reach any of its objectives before daylight, and had the greatest difficulty in extricating itself under constant air attack in the next few days. The raid on Barce by the Long Range Desert Group, under Major Easonsmith accompanied by Major Peniakoff ('Popski' of 'Popski's Private Army' fame), was more successful. They did a good deal of damage in Barce itself, destroyed or damaged most of the 30 aircraft on the airfield and withdrew with few casualties to men or vehicles. However they were spotted on their return and relentlessly pursued by Italian aircraft, until by the evening of the 14th they had only one truck and two jeeps left. The attack on Gialo by a motor battalion of the Sudan Defence Force had penetrated to both the old and the new forts, but came under heavy air attack before it had got further than the western part of the oasis. Ammunition had run low and, as the failure of the other operations had removed the need for a base there, the force was withdrawn to Kufra just as it was preparing to renew the attack on Gialo itself.

Montgomery had had no responsibility for these operations and viewed the whole affair with disfavour. He was not surprised when they failed, and there is little doubt that they influenced him against attempting anything similar in the long pursuit from El Alamein to Tunis. GHQ in Cairo considered that they affected Rommel by making him keep Italian troops tied down to the defence of his rear areas; but there is no evidence to support this. The usual instructions were, it is true, issued for everyone to be prepared to deal with such operations and a small detachment of Italian armoured cars was sent to Siwa.

The day which saw the withdrawal of the raiding party from Tobruk, the Joint Intelligence Committee in Cairo drew up an appreciation of the enemy's situation. Although Rommel was in no position to attack, they thought he would not withdraw. He could not find a better defensive position and, if our airfields were brought nearer to Tobruk, he would probably be unable to use the port. Withdrawal would therefore only make his supply and reinforcement problem even worse. In spite of his difficulties he would probably have accumulated enough supplies by the end of October for three or four weeks of active operations. If, as was likely, he gave priority to supplies and equipment over reinforcements, the German 22nd Division was unlikely to arrive before the beginning of November. His tank strength might increase by 20 to 25 tanks a week. In the air he would probably concentrate on improving his defence with fighters. The committee finally came to the conclusion that he was unlikely to launch a major attack again until early in November.

Next day Montgomery held a conference for all divisional commanders and their chief staff officers, at which he explained his plan for the operation, which was to be called 'Lightfoot'. His aim was to trap the enemy and destroy him where he was by attacks on both flanks, the main blow being in the north. Leese's 30th Corps was to force a gap there, through which the armoured divisions of Lumsden's 10th Corps would pass in order that the Corps should 'position itself on ground of its own choosing' astride the enemy's supply routes. Rommel's tanks would then attack and be destroyed. While this was going on, Horrocks 13th Corps would attack in the south and draw the enemy tanks off, in the hope of weakening the opposition to 10th Corps.

Montgomery stressed that it was essential for the leading armoured brigades to be in their deployment areas ready to fight at dawn of the first day. They were not to become embroiled in fighting in the early hours while moving there. 30th Corps' operations were to be designed to ensure that 10th Corps could pass unopposed through the gaps made in the enemy minefields. The latter was then to 'pivot' on Miteiriya Ridge, to be held by its own New Zealand Division, and swing right round in an anti-clockwise direction until the Corps was positioned astride the enemy supply routes. What happened after that would depend on Rommel's reactions. He might attack 10th Corps directly: if he did not, the latter would be able to attack the enemy armour from the flank. In either case, once his armour was destroyed, the rest of Rommel's army would be rounded up without difficulty.

This was the plan towards which all training must be directed. Although the outline of the plan could be and was revealed as far down the chain of command as brigade headquarters by the end of the month, secrecy about the actual date was essential. Some indication had to be given, however, if everything was to be ready in time.

When Churchill had left Cairo on August 23rd he had expected the new offensive to be launched in the September full moon period, about the 22nd. This was the latest he had been prepared to accept in view of both of the requirements of Operation 'Torch', the projected landings in North Africa, and the urgent needs of Malta. Final decisions on the former were proving difficult to achieve.

The Americans had suddenly evinced a dislike of carrying out any of their landings within the Mediterranean, and this was bound to lead to delay. At the end of August Churchill was still hoping they would land on October 14th, but was beginning to realise that the end of that month was more likely. By the end of Alam el Halfa he had realised that it could not be before then. It was considered most important that Montgomery should have achieved a clear victory by that time, as this would go far towards influencing the French in North Africa to welcome rather than oppose the Anglo-American landings.

The other factor pressing for an early date was the situation of Malta. Petrol was essential in order to maintain the Air Force and naval air activity, both defensive and offensive; but stocks would only last until November 22nd. Food would last until early December, unless stocks were reduced by bombing, but if it was to be distributed in time, more food must arrive by the middle of November. To get a convoy there by then meant that the landing grounds near Benghazi must be in British hands by early November. The full moon period of September would have met both the needs of 'Torch' and of Malta, but a month's postponement would be running things fine for both.

It was quite clear to Montgomery that there could be no question of attacking in the September full moon, only a fortnight after Alam el Halfa. The next full moon fell on October 24th. Could he attack without a full moon and, if he could, would he in any case be ready before then? It was clear that the principal problem would be that of clearing gaps through the minefields and getting the armour out beyond. The infantry attack to capture the enemy's minefields and defences, and the work of clearing and marking the minefield gaps could not be done in daylight in the desert. It was hazardous also to try and pass the armour in daylight through narrow lanes from which they would emerge in single file. Moonlight was going to be essential for the difficult task of finding, clearing and marking the gaps through the minefields and the lanes leading to them. It was going to be hard enough to complete all that had to be done in one night. If the period of moonlight was restricted, it would be impossible. Montgomery decided therefore that he must start the battle on the eve of the full moon, giving him the best conditions for the first night and acceptable ones for the following week. In any case the reorganisation, re-equipment and training of 10th Corps could not be complete much before the middle of October, and time had to be allowed for the final deployment. He therefore chose the night of October 23rd and decided that he could not accept an earlier date.

Alexander realised that this would be unpopular in London and visited Montgomery to discuss it. The latter convinced him and, confident of the strength of his personal position after Alam el Halfa, said he would resign his command rather than change. Churchill forced the issue by sending a telegram to Alexander on September 17th, as soon as Brooke had escaped for a few days' leave to shoot grouse in Yorkshire. He said that he was anxiously awaiting some account of Alexander's intentions. He had accepted the fourth week of September, but had now been told that Alam el Halfa, 'which greatly weakened the enemy, had caused delay in regrouping, etc.'. He said that he could not make other decisions without knowing which week it was to fall in. Alexander replied with the decision that Montgomery had arrived at and the cogent reasons for it. This upset Churchill who, as a result, had a somewhat acrimonious telephone conversation with Brooke in Yorkshire, who had not seen Alexander's reply. Having seen. it next day, he telephoned Churchill again and told him that he supported Alexander, which did not prevent the Prime Minister from urging Alexander to hasten the date. Churchill continued to brood over this unpalatable delay and conjured up visions of Rommel erecting impenetrable defences in the meanwhile. Two days later, the 22nd, Eisenhower decided that November 8th should be the D-Day for Operation 'Torch' and the Cabinet agreed. Next day Brooke was faced with the draft of another telegram which the Prime Minister intended to send to Alexander. After an argument in which Brooke said it showed lack of confidence in Alexander, and Churchill held forth on his usual theme of generals always wanting everything perfect before they would do anything, which only allowed the enemy to do the same, a compromise was reached on a watered-down version. This suggested that enemy defences, instead of being a crust which could be penetrated in one night, might be '25 miles of fortifications, with blasted rock, gun-pits and machine-gun posts' and that the infantry would find it hard to clear a way for the tanks through this.

'No doubt you are thinking about this' he concluded 'and how so to broaden your front of attack as to make your superior numbers felt' – and there the matter rested.

The principal object of training was to develop a sound and well-practised method to cover first the capture of the enemy's minefield area and the defences immediately covering it: secondly, and starting as soon as possible, to clear lanes through the minefields wide enough for vehicles to pass, marking them and the routes leading to them clearly enough to be seen in the dark amid the clouds of dust which bursting shells and moving tanks would create: finally to pass a vast mass of vehicles through in the right order, while the infantry divisions made themselves secure against enemy counter-attack in daylight. All this had to be completed in about ten hours of darkness.

The first step was to set up 8th Army minefield clearance school, first under Major Peter Moore of the Royal Engineers and then under Major A. R. Currie of the New Zealand Engineers, which trained teams from 56 different engineer units before the battle. Hopes were also placed on mechanical means. Using the same basic idea as was being developed in England as the 'Flail', some old Matilda tanks had been converted locally and were known as 'Scorpions'. The initiative in this had been taken within 30th Corps after 23rd Armoured Brigade had lost a great many tanks on minefields in July. The venture had the enthusiastic support of Brigadier Kisch, the Chief Engineer of the Army, and 24 had been ordered after a pilot model had given a successful demonstration for the benefit of senior officers. Major Drury of the Royal Tank Regiment was placed in charge, but was beset with difficulties, due partly to mechanical troubles and partly to the demands of secrecy which limited trials both to eliminate the troubles and practise the technique. The original idea had been for a whole troop of them to operate together, echelonned and overlapping each other. This would have made a gap which needed no further widening. The dust created by the action of the flail caused the engine to overheat and made it impossible for the other Scorpions to keep direction. Both

10th and 30th Corps therefore refused to rely on them, as they feared that they would block the gaps they made. 7th Armoured Division in 13th Corps alone tried to make full use of them. The other two corps were to rely on the primitive method of 'prodding' with bayonets or specially made implements and on mine detectors, as far as their availability would allow – 499 were available to the Army, of which 202 went to 30th Corps, 180 to 10th Corps and 117 to 13th Corps. 88,775 lamps were issued and 120 miles of marking tape, most of both to 30th Corps.

The problem of training the divisions of 30th Corps who were to launch the initial assault was complicated by the fact that two of them, the Australian and the South African, had to continue to hold the front line. In the former each brigade was taken out of the line for a week at a time for intensive training. This was helped by an arrangement by which 51st Highland sent a brigade at a time to gain experience under the Australians. The Highlanders had a large training area within reach of their reserve position at Alam el Halfa in which four major rehearsals were held, the first on September 26th, and three in October before the final move forward. Unfortunately in one of these several casualties were caused by their own artillery fire.

Pienaar's 1st South African Division, which had been in the line continuously since the beginning of July, relieved its 2nd Brigade from September 16th to October 5th, when it returned to set 3rd Brigade free for training. Pienaar's own old brigade, the 1st, was not going to take part in the actual attack, and stayed in the line all the time. Tuker's 4th Indian Division, which had no major part to play apart from holding Ruweisat Ridge, was stripped of its transport and told to carry out individual training as best it could.

13th Corps could do little about training. Not only did it have to hold its front, but also had to carry out an operation to try and get rid of an awkward enemy salient at the western end of Munassib. This task was given to Frith's 131st Brigade of 44th Division to execute on the night of September 29th. It resulted in an expensive failure, much of the cause of which can be attributed to the lack of experience and training of the division. Unlike its more fortunate

companion, the 51st Highland, it had been rushed up to the
front and thrown into operations without a single day's
training since it had arrived in the Middle East. Inadequate
previous patrolling led to the considerable artillery support
being wasted on empty desert, while the difficulties of a
long approach march, culminating in soft broken ground,
had neither been fully realised nor allowed for.

The division had not only lost its 133rd Brigade to 10th
Corps but its reconnaissance battalion and all its Bren
carrier platoons had been formed into a special unit as a
minefield clearance task force under 22nd Armoured Brigade. During October the two remaining brigades took it
in turn to hold the eastern end of Munassib, the one out
of the line carrying out a rehearsal of an attack on a minefield.

7th Armoured Division also had its training difficulties,
4th Light Armoured Brigade, now commanded by Roddick
instead of Carr, not being relieved until October 18th by
the Free French, leaving no time for either of them to train.
22nd Armoured Brigade was however free to train in its own
area and carried out three exercises in October, the last in
co-operation with 131st Brigade.

10th Corps had no problems of holding the line, but the
training of its armoured divisions was hampered both by
problems of reorganisation and of re-equipment. All three
divisions had to receive and absorb new motor infantry brigades. 1st Armoured Division was best off in this respect,
although 7th Motor Brigade did not join until September
23rd, and it was able to start forming its minefield clearance
task force under 2nd Rifle Brigade on October 4th. After
this the division moved to a training area west of Wadi
Natrun, where it was able to hold three exercises before
moving up to its assembly area. 8th Armoured Division, as
has already been related, broke up at the end of September.
Its brigades, 24th Armoured Brigade and the recently converted 133rd Lorried Infantry, had been able to do hardly
any training before they joined 10th Armoured Division.
Both were in the throes of re-equipment and the second had
to face a host of unfamiliar problems as a result of its con-
version. The 10th's own armoured brigade, the 8th, was

little better off. It was not until October 12th that it was told that it would get 33 new Sherman tanks instead of Grants: 15 were issued on the 17th, and the remainder did not arrive until the day of the battle itself. Each regiment was to get 11, but they had little time for training before the battle and many important bits of equipment were missing and did not arrive until the very last moment.

Although officially in 10th Corps, the New Zealand Division was to start the battle under the 30th, under whose command it in fact remained throughout. It had a comparatively uninterrupted period of training south of its rest area near Burg el Arab, and carried out several exercises designed to practise passing 9th Armoured Brigade through the infantry on the final objective.

It was largely these problems of training the armoured divisions which prompted Montgomery to reconsider his plan and make it less ambitious, at any rate as far as the action of 10th Corps was concerned. On October 6th he revised his orders. Under the new plan 30th Corps was to destroy the enemy's infantry while 10th Corps held off his armour. Rommel would not be able to afford to see his infantry systematically worn away, and would be forced to attack with his tanks to save them. This would involve attacking 10th Corps on 'ground of its own choosing'. If the Corps were not able to destroy the enemy armour early on, it was to be manœuvred in such a way as to prevent Rommel from interfering with 30th Corps' 'crumbling' operations. In addition opportunities might occur for it to help 30th Corps by itself conducting operations on the front of 9th Australian Division, or to the south of Miteiriya Ridge on the west flank of the New Zealanders. The general pattern of the battle was to follow three stages. The first was the 'break-in' to enemy positions on the first night. The second, the 'crumbling' operation, was to start at dawn next day, and great emphasis was laid on the need to start these operations then. Thereafter there was no firm plan, but everyone was to be ready to take instant advantage of any weakening of the opposition. The enemy was to be given no respite and there were to be no long pauses to allow him to recover balance.

Within this plan Leese's objectives were altered slightly to avoid some of the stronger enemy defences near the coast. His task involved an attack with four divisions, from right to left Morshead's 9th Australian, Wimberley's 51st Highland, Freyberg's 2nd New Zealand and Pienaar's 1st South African, on a front of four and a half miles to a depth on the right of five and a quarter and on the left of two and three-quarter miles. This was to make it possible for Lumsden to advance on two lanes through the area captured and establish his corps by dawn west of the enemy's main defensive positions, while Leese began his 'crumbling' operations against the infantry divisions remaining in the defences. Horrocks had a subsidiary part to play. Apart from a number of diversions, he was to attack on a narrow front with Harding's 7th Armoured and Hughes' 44th Division 'well to the south of Ruweisat Ridge', in order to mislead the enemy into thinking that this was the main thrust and to keep 21st Panzer Division down in the south. The attack was to be accompanied by operations to clear Himeimat and the Taqa Plateau and was not to be pressed home unless resistance proved to be unexpectedly weak. In that case Harding was to be directed towards Daba. Diversionary operations were also to be carried out by the 1st Special Air Service Regiment behind the enemy lines and the Royal Navy were to simulate a landing near Daba.

The general policy for the Royal Air Force was to gain air supremacy first and then, once the battle had started, to devote most of its effort to direct support. A short, intense period of attack on the enemy landing grounds at Daba and Fuka was made early in October, when the Luftwaffe, grounded by rain, lost 30 aircraft. The air offensive proper however did not begin until the night of October 18th, when night attacks on Tobruk were intensified and night-fighters attacked the railway. Next day attacks were made on the landing grounds at Daba, on troop concentrations in the northern and central sectors of the front and on traffic on the road and railway between Mersa Matruh and Sidi Barrani. Tobruk and the Daba landing grounds were again attacked during the night, and on the 20th operations were extended to include Fuka landing ground. All these targets were attacked again and again right up to the start of the battle, attacks on the night of the 21st being switched to targets in Crete.

It was clearly impossible to imagine that the enemy would not appreciate that a major attack was soon to be launched. The only hope of surprise lay in misleading him as to the date when Montgomery would be ready and the sector in which the main blow would come. It was thought that the enemy had six sources of information available to him. First, the appearance of new or improved tracks; secondly variations in the density of vehicles, particularly tracked ones, in different areas; thirdly alterations in the size and number of 'dumps' of stores, and finally improvements in means of water supply, particularly new pipelines. All these could be spotted or photographed from the air. In addition the enemy could gain information from alterations in the density of wireless traffic, from agents in the Delta and from interrogation of prisoners. A comprehensive deception plan was therefore put in train under the direction of Lieutenant-Colonel Richardson. The construction of new tracks in the northern sector was left till the last possible moment, particularly the final sections. While 10th Corps was training round Wadi Natrun, the bulk of its transport with that of the New Zealand and Highland Divisions was collected in its final assembly area, reinforced by dummy vehicles to the number of those still training. When the divisions actually moved into these areas, dummies were re-erected in the training areas. There was therefore no apparent change. The positions in which the infantry divisions were to spend the day of the attack itself were dug and camouflaged also a month before. Dumps were concealed in two ways: by extending existing dumps which had not been concealed, the extensions being gradual and hidden as far as possible; and by building stacks of stores to look like lorries or bivouac tents which were already there. In this way 3,000 tons of ammunition were dumped round El Imayid station, 420 tons of engineer stores near El Alamein station, 2,000 tons of petrol in old slit trenches in the same area; 600 tons each of other supplies and ordnance stores were also dumped. The existing 8-inch diameter water pipe from Alexandria was replaced by a 10-inch pipe, laid and buried at night, the old pipe being left on the surface. A new water point near El Alamein station was concealed and not used until the battle had started. In addition to these passive measures, the Royal Air Force concentrated their fighter defence over the northern sector in the last few days before the battle.

To deal with wireless interception, 8th Armoured divisional signals were used to continue wireless traffic in 10th Corps' training area after the Corps had moved. In addition, throughout the Army, call-signs and frequencies were often changed and long periods of wireless silence were interspersed with periods devoted to sending training messages.

To defeat agents who might pick up indiscretions, nobody to whom the plan for the battle had been revealed was allowed to leave 8th Army area on any pretext. Regimental officers, other than commanding officers, were not told the plan till the 21st, and the men not until the 22nd or 23rd. Unobtrusive arrangements were made to see that those who were due to go on leave in the few days before the 23rd were those who had been chosen to be 'Left out of Battle'. Early in October the whole Army was put on to hard rations for a few days and the fresh ration contract in the Delta stopped for a time, so that a repetition later in the month should cause no comment. On October 6th, Montgomery issued a strict order that no visitors were to be allowed into 8th Army's area without his personal sanction.

To prevent prisoners from giving anything away, only those troops actually holding the front line were allowed to patrol. Engineers from further back, who might have seen the vast scale of preparations in progress, were not allowed to reconnoitre the minefields they were to have to clear. Even on the day of the attack it was forbidden to take marked maps into the forward area.

Although traffic was strictly controlled in the northern sector, movement of vehicles in the south was encouraged and other steps were taken to make the enemy think it was to be the scene of the main thrust. Dummy artillery positions, badly camouflaged, were constructed at the east end of Munassib and dummy dumps and administrative areas were

built down in the south. A dummy pipeline, complete with
pump-houses and reservoirs, left the real water point west
of Ruweisea station and led to a dummy water point four
miles east of Samaket Gaballa. Work started on September
26th and progressed at a rate which indicated that it would
be completed early in November. When 10th Corps moved
forward the initial moves were in daylight to a staging
area well to the south behind 13th Corps.

The first move in this final forward deployment started
in daylight on October 18th, and most were complete by
dawn on the 23rd.

All the physical preparations were as complete as they could
be. They would be of no avail if the troops were not in good
fighting trim. Montgomery had applied himself to this problem with especial care. Changes in command were not
confined to the higher echelons and a good deal of weeding
out went on. The Army Commander soon began to impress
his personality on all and sundry wherever he went, aided
by his unconventional headgear. On September 14th he had
issued a special order about morale, stressing the need for
physical as well as mental fitness to get soldiers tough and
hard. It was followed on October 6th by another about
leadership, this time concentrating on the soldier's duty
never to surrender. There is no doubt that there was a
general feeling of confidence and determination as the date
of the battle approached, although feelings differed by formations and individuals. Probably the keenest were the Highland Division. They had St Valéry to avenge and had not
seen a shot fired since the division had re-formed after the
fall of France. They had been specially favoured since arrival
and represented the cream of Highland fighting stock. The
Australians had been in the line since mid-July, but before
that the 9th Division had seen little action, having been
relieved in Tobruk before 'Crusader'. It was tough and
full of fight. The New Zealanders too had been fortunate to
miss the Gazala battles of the summer. Since 'Crusader'
they had been out of the line until coming up to Matruh in
the retreat. Since then they had had several unhappy experiences, but they were tough, seasoned and hard-bitten veter-

ans except for Currie's armoured brigade, which was new to battle, the 3rd Hussars alone having fought before, although not since Crete. 1st South African had been at Gazala, but had taken little part in the main battle. Since their arrival in the desert after their spectacular and victorious march from Kenya to Addis Abbaba, they had seldom had a really satisfactory battle. They had been in the line at El Alamein without relief since the beginning of July and were not as fresh as they might have been. 4th Indian and 50th Divisions were desert veterans, but were not called upon to take part in the main attack, the latter particularly having not yet recovered from its losses of the summer. 44th Division were undoubtedly the unlucky ones. They had been 'mucked about' to no mean tune since they had arrived. The attacks which first 132nd and then 131st Brigade had launched had been hopeless failures. They had lost 133rd Brigade and were now to play a subsidiary role to 7th Armoured Division in the south.

7th Armoured Division, the old faithful, shorn of its motor brigade, at the bottom of the list for tank replacements, could be forgiven if it felt that it was unpopular with all these new arrivals from England. It was, however, blessed with two exceptional commanders, John Harding and 'Pip' Roberts. It had never liked the coastal area and was glad to be well away on its own in the south. Its task was not an easy one, but the division had no doubt that it could do it as well as any other.

Beneath the surface all was not entirely serene among the generals. When Montgomery had changed his plan, he had also ordered that, if 30th Corps had not yet reached their final objectives on time, 10th Corps was to fight its own way through. This was a very different prospect from that of waiting for 30th Corps to clear a way right through the main defensive position and then deploying into an area clear of mines and fixed defences. Neither Lumsden nor his divisional commanders regarded it as a feasible proposition. They were not alone in this. The three Dominion divisional commanders, Freyberg, Morshead and Pienaar, made it clear to Leese that they had no confidence that the armoured divisions could succeed in breaking out so soon.

They foresaw attempts to do so as possibly leading to disaster to the armour, for which they themselves would suffer later. They thought that the infantry attack should continue for longer before the break-out was attempted. 30th Corps soon came to suspect that 10th Corps were not even seriously intending to try to break out. Faced with this, Leese told Montgomery, who reiterated that 10th Corps *must* pass through 30th Corps at dawn on the first day. No doubt he was influenced by memories of France in the First World War, when long pauses between successive infantry attacks were merely used by the enemy to strengthen the opposition to them. He must have realised too that he had insufficient infantry to develop his 'break-in' any deeper. In Lumsden's two armoured divisions therefore confidence in the outcome may have been slender. 1st Armoured Division were all veterans and had the advantage that their old divisional commander now commanded the Corps. In 10th Armoured Division 8th Armoured Brigade's only action had been their unsatisfactory brush with 15th Panzer on the second day of Alam el Halfa: 24th Armoured Brigade had never seen a shot fired, nor since Dunkirk had 133rd Lorried Infantry Brigade, which suffered the further disadvantage that it had only recently been snatched away from its division and pushed into the unfamiliar role of lorried infantry with inadequate time to reorganise and train.

For most people the last few days before the battle were taken up with the business of moving forward to the final area. For the commanders and staffs of higher formations there was little now to do, certainly nothing which could influence the outcome. So the sensible ones relaxed and did not go round fussing their subordinates either. De Guingand broke all the secrecy rules by going to Alexandria for two nights a few days before the battle. Most people read books or played cards, or just slept: almost all wrote letters, which many thought might be their last. For almost everyone, but particularly for the infantry divisions of 30th Corps due to take part in the assault, the 23rd was a long, trying day. The infantry had to spend it immobile and hidden, crouched in their slit trenches which they could not leave even for natural purposes. There was nothing to do but wait. It was best not to think about the battle, but it was never out of one's thoughts. This long hot wait in cramped idleness told hardest on those facing their first encounter with the enemy. The veteran took it with that mixture of cynicism, fatalism and outward calm which is characteristic of his race and his profession, and which so often conceals much deeper feelings than he would admit to.

Montgomery himself appeared to have no doubts. His tactical headquarters was moved up to the beach just north of El Alamein station, close to those of both Lumsden and Leese. Montgomery had already issued his confident order of the day, asking the army to pray that 'the Lord mighty in battle' would give them victory. He briefed the Press in the morning and drove with de Guingand to his tactical headquarters in time for a cup of tea at half past four. Then he settled down to a book and went to bed earlier than usual after dinner, in the hope of getting to sleep before the guns thundered out.

There was no sign that the enemy had any inkling that the attack was imminent, but there had been two scares. On the night of October 11th two Highlanders had been missing from a patrol on the Australian front. Calm was restored a few days later when the official report of the German 164th Division on their interrogation was itself captured, proving that they had given nothing away. There was a last-minute scare on the 23rd itself, when a report reached 30th Corps that an officer and a non-commissioned officer of the 5th Camerons had been missing since nine o'clock on the 22nd. However, at half past six that evening, 8th Army intelligence told Montgomery that all the evidence pointed to the fact that the enemy were not expecting an attack that night – and they were right.

6 WITHOUT HOPE

In strong contrast to the air of renewed confidence and vigour in 8th Army the Panzer Armee Afrika looked forward to the next round without hope, with resignation and in some cases with despair, accentuated by the absence of its inspiring commander. When the Battle of Alam el Halfa came to an end with the Germans and Italians back in the old British front line in the south, Rommel had no illusions about what lay in store for him. His doctor, Professor Hörster, insisted that he must go to Europe and have a cure and a rest for several weeks at least, and arrangements had already been made for his temporary relief by General Stumme, fifty-six-year-old ex-commander of Rommel's old 7th Panzer Division, who had also commanded a corps on the Russian front. Rommel had less than a fortnight in which to get his army organised to meet the attack by Montgomery which he thought would come in four to six weeks' time. He moved 15th Panzer Division up to the coast for a week's rest first and then to the area six miles SSW of Sidi Abd el Rahman. 21st Panzer Division stayed in the south, but pulled back to the north-west of Gebel Kalakh. De Stefanis' XX Corps was split up, Littorio being grouped with 15th Panzer in the north and Ariete with 21st in the south. Trieste was in reserve in the northern sector south of 90th Light, which was on the coast east of Daba.

Navarrini's XXI Corps continued to hold the northern sector as far down as just south of Ruweisat Ridge, corresponding exactly with the sector of the British 30th Corps. Two battalions of Ramcke's brigade with some Bersaglieri held the narrow sector from the coast to the railway, 164th Division being responsible for the concave front as far south as Kidney Ridge. Trento with a German parachute battalion held Miteiriya Ridge, and Bologna faced east to the south of it down to Ruweisat Ridge, held by two German parachute battalions. To the south Orsi's X Corps had Brescia with two more German parachute battalions opposite 50th Division, and Folgore held the front from south of Munassib down to Himeimat, which with the Taqa plateau was the responsibility of the newly arrived Pavia Division. In the soft ground to the south Kiel group and 33rd Reconnaissance Unit continued to guard the flank.

Previously Rommel's aim had been to force the British to fight mobile battles, confident in his own superiority at that game. He was realistic enough to see that this would no longer do. The relative strengths of mobile forces, always numerically in favour of the British, were now getting to a state when they were too unequal for numbers to be outweighed by superior skill. 8th Army was receiving massive additions to its mechanised strength, while such reinforcements as Rommel did receive came without vehicles. This made them, in his words, 'as good as useless in the open desert'. The overwhelming British air superiority and Rommel's permanent shortage of petrol were the other two reasons why he was forced to base his defence on a static fortified line, defended by infantry making the fullest possible use of minefields. He had to accept that this sort of battle would make it possible for the British to use their artillery to fullest effect and to exploit the qualities of the Australian and New Zealand infantry, of whom Rommel was a great admirer. The immobility of his infantry made it essential for Rommel to prevent a break-through at all costs. He believed that 8th Army would attack simultaneously at several points and then try to develop the most favourable into a break-through. He therefore decided that any penetration would have to be eliminated by immediate counter-attack to prevent such development. The main defensive positions were to be made capable of holding out against the heaviest attack long enough for the Panzer divisions to come to their aid, even if delayed by air attack.

One of the first steps to make certain of this was a deliberate policy of 'sandwiching' German and Italian troops right down to the level of battalions. For instance, although their sectors were nominally separate, in fact 164th German and Trento Italian divisions completely overlapped each other. German and Italian headquarters were sited close to-

gether in order that the former might 'make suggestions'
to the latter.

In the orders which Rommel gave just before he left he
went into considerable detail as to how the defences were
to be organised. Existing forward minefields were to be held
only by section posts, some actually in the minefields and
some behind. These were to be regarded merely as a forward or outpost position. About a mile behind there was to
be a wide minefield belt, on the rear edge of which the main
defensive position was to be built. A battalion holding such
a position was normally to have one company with 50-mm.
anti-tank guns in the forward position and the rest in the
main position behind. An average battalion sector would be
1,500 yards wide and 5,000 yards deep. Rommel rightly
foresaw that the standard British type of infantry division
attack would waste most of its artillery and infantry effort
and its time on attacking the forward positions. Not only
would all surprise about the direction and extent of the
attack be lost by the time the main positions were reached,
but the whole impetus would have died down also. Any
attempt to pass mobile forces through at that stage would
bring them up against the main position with its strong anti-
tank defence which, he hoped, would have been missed by
the intense artillery fire close to the attacking infantry. This
pattern of British attack on German defences was to be
repeated again throughout the Second World War, as it had
been in the First. Not for nothing had Rommel been the
author of the German Army's manual of infantry tactics.

Having set the pattern for the defence, Rommel prepared
to hand over to Stumme who arrived on September 19th.
His was not an enviable task. He could not hope to equal
Rommel in the eyes of the Panzer Armee and knew that in
any case he would not himself have a free hand. Not only
had the orders been issued, but to his consternation Rommel
announced that, if the British launched a major attack, he
would immediately return. Most of the principal staff officers
were sick, Gause the Chief of Staff was to leave immediately,
Westphal had jaundice and Mellenthin amoebic dysentery.
The Afrika Korps and two German divisions had had new
commanders within the preceding fortnight. General von

Thoma had taken over the Korps, General von Randow had arrived to take the place of von Bismarck in 21st Panzer and General Graf von Sponeck had succeeded Kleemann in 90th Light Division. He was fortunate that the other two, von Vaerst of 15th Panzer and Lungerhausen of 164th Division remained. On the day of his arrival a conference on the logistic situation was held with Cavallero. Rommel demanded that shipments in September should be completed to 30,000 tons and increased in October to 35,000. Every single vehicle that could be got across the Mediterranean must be sent. He could not hope to fight a successful defensive battle with less than eight daily issues of ammunition, 2,000 miles of petrol for every vehicle and a month's rations. Promises were given as usual that every effort would be made to meet his demands, but when he left Derna on the 23rd he had few illusions about the extent to which they would be.

Next day he saw Mussolini and once more represented the urgency of action to improve the supply and transport situation of his army. Both there and in his interview with Hitler and Goering a few days later he got the impression that they thought he was exaggerating his difficulties. Several times before he had done what had been logistically impossible by all the rules. They had no doubt he could do it again. Had he not himself belittled talk of supply difficulties and described them as the small-minded quibbling of quartermasters? Rommel did not mince his words. He painted a vivid picture of the overwhelming air superiority of the British and of its effects, which did not endear him to Goering. He repeated his minimum needs for the logistic support of a successful defence and was fobbed off with promises of powered ferries, Tiger tanks and Nebelwerfer rockets, none of which could in fact reach the Army by the time the attack would certainly take place.

It was with a heavy heart that Rommel went off for his cure to Semmering in the mountains of Austria. There he brooded over the influence the great industrial power of America was going to have, which only a successful submarine campaign in the Atlantic could prevent from becoming a decisive factor in preventing German victory. His thoughts were with the Panzer Armee, and the letter which came from Stumme and Westphal did little for his peace of mind. Although work on the minefields and defences was going ahead fast and for the moment there was little activity either on the ground or in the air near the front line, there was no doubt that 8th Army and the Desert Air Force were getting appreciably stronger every day. Air raids on Tobruk continued every night and the toll of shipping mounted. A large number of ships had been sunk in September and seven more were hit by aerial torpedoes between the 1st and 23rd of October. Not all the cargo was lost, but little of it reached the front before the battle. Although the supply situation improved, it did not look like reaching Rommel's minimum demands.

The absence of their leader weighed on the minds of the Germans of the Panzer Armee. Visions of capturing Egypt had faded from the imagination of even the most optimistic. There was little improvement in health and flies became a greater scourge than ever. Most of the Italians, except for comparatively new arrivals like Folgore, had largely lost interest and were longing for the end of the war. Differences between them and the Germans, originating at the top, spread down to every level as the policy of 'sandwiching' the two was put into effect. However all worked hard on defences as their own survival depended on them. Particular attention was paid to minefields and to sowing anti-personnel mines and booby-traps among the anti-tank mines. A complete new main defence line behind the original front line was taking shape in the northern sector by mid-October, but in the south work was restricted to strengthening the original British first and second minefields, now known to 8th Army as 'January' and 'February'. The artillery kept quiet, partly to save ammunition, but chiefly to avoid giving away their positions, which had now mostly been set back out of range of the British field artillery. The guns which did fire moved beforehand to temporary positions away from their normal ones and moved again when their task was over. The infantry also had a quiet time at night as they did little or no patrolling. As a result they had only the vaguest idea of what was going on beyond 'no man's land', which in some cases stretched for a mile or two between the foremost minefields of either side. The Panzer and Italian armoured divisions remained stationary. They had to be ready to move quickly if the front were threatened, as 21st Panzer was ready to do when 131st Brigade attacked Folgore at the end of September. By day they could get to work on their vehicles or practise gunnery and battle drill. The two Panzer divisions now totalled 220 tanks, of which most were the old Mark III with the short 50-mm. gun, while the Italians had 318 medium and 21 light tanks.

October 23rd was a day like any other for the Panzer Armee, and they were settling down for another quiet night as usual when, at twenty minutes to nine by their time, the whole front suddenly leapt into flame and shells rained over endlessly, aimed at the artillery but switching to the forward infantry positions after the first twenty minutes.

7 THE FIRST BLOW

October 23rd – 24th

At twenty minutes to ten by Egypt Summer Time all the artillery which 8th Army could bring to bear opened an intense counter-battery programme which served the double purpose of concealing the infantry's final move to the start line and dealing the enemy's artillery a crippling blow. Leese had 426 field and 48 medium guns to deal with the 232 field, 40 medium and 24 heavy enemy guns on his front. Nearly 80 of these could only be reached by the mediums, which concentrated 96 shells in two minutes on each battery in turn, firing 1,800 rounds in this way before zero hour. The enemy's response was feeble and, according to the gunners, it was not until four in the morning that their counterparts began to fire back on any considerable scale. Some of the infantry would deny this.

The tremendous bombardment gave a great fillip to the spirits of the infantry who were marching forward and shaking out into their final formation for the attack. There were differences of detail here and there, but the general pattern was the same from the extreme right of the Australians to the left of the South Africans. Close behind the artillery barrage, which soon obscured everything in its area with dust and smoke, the leading companies advanced in line, two or three yards between each man, at a pace of 100 yards in two minutes until they reached the edge of the first minefield. In most cases this was about a mile and a half away.

For the first hour therefore little was likely to happen. Behind the leading lines the bright moonlight showed the infantry and sappers in steel helmets, cardigans and shorts moving slowly and steadily forward as if on an exercise. Only the tremendous roar of the guns behind and the constant 'crump' of shells in front marked the difference. To help them keep direction searchlights at fixed points directed their beams straight up into the clear night sky and light anti-aircraft guns fired tracer shells at intervals on fixed lines forward.

After the long suspense it was a relief to be off at last. At first there was little in the way of opposition, few shells, hardly any bullets and no mines until the first field was reached. Perhaps it was all going to be easy and the qualms and fears, which had been gnawing away all day, were soon dispelled. This wave of carefree optimism was to be shattered for most of the infantry when they came up against the main positions further on later in the night. Then everything seemed to happen at once. Bullets whined and cracked around them, and shells 'crumped' as they struggled to get through the wire and hoped there were no mines among it. The orderly surge forward became a desperate struggle to keep up, get going again and try to keep track of where their friends were and what they were doing.

Leese's task was first to capture and secure a bridgehead through the enemy's minefields and defences before dawn; secondly to help Lumsden's tanks pass through it, and finally to exploit the 'break-in' on both flanks. The bridgehead was to extend from two miles north of Kidney Ridge, the responsibility of Morshead's Australians, through the east edge of it south-eastwards to the north-west end of Miteiriya Ridge, these two points marking the flanks of Wimberley's objectives. On his left Freyberg was to advance 1,000 yards beyond the first three miles of the ridge, while Pienaar came up in line with him for the remaining three miles of it. On the whole front the attack was to be carried out in two phases, the first being the capture of the enemy's forward positions, in most cases rather over a mile behind the forward edge of the first enemy minefield. This was known as 'Red' line, and the artillery programme was timed on the assumption that it would be reached at five minutes to midnight, two hours after the infantry had started. There would then be a pause of an hour before the attack was resumed over the two miles to the final objective, known as 'Blue' line, which would include the enemy's main defences. If all went according to plan, these should be captured by a quarter to three.

In the three hours left before dawn the infantry would

dig in and organise themselves to meet counter-attacks with their anti-tank guns, mortars and machine-guns, while Lumsden's tanks, starting at two o'clock from their assembly areas behind, would pass through the gaps their own engineers had cleared and out into the unknown beyond. Richards' tanks of 23rd Armoured Brigade with the infantry divisions and Currie's 9th Armoured Brigade with the New Zealanders were 'to be used as necessary in order to ensure the capture of the bridgehead at all costs'. They were not to be used in formations smaller than a squadron nor were they to be launched against uncleared minefields: 'a proportion should be kept available to meet counter-attacks at dawn.'

When they had organised themselves on their final object-ives, all divisions were to send fighting patrols forward to attack enemy guns and were to do all they could to help the armoured divisions through. Once daylight had broken the Australians were to be prepared for a further advance to the north and the New Zealanders were to exploit five miles southwards as far as the enemy positions north-west of Deir el Shein, the South Africans converging towards them at the same time. The western flank of this exploitation, which appears to have been Leese's interpretation of 'crumbling', would be protected by Lumsden's left flank. Emphasis was to be laid on the part that could be played by pockets of troops who might themselves be isolated, and there was to be no question of surrender by anyone who was not wounded. As if to complete the similarity with operations of the First World War, 'a limited number of pigeons was issued'.

With Morshead's Australians on the right the whole oper-ation went almost entirely according to plan. Godfrey's 24th Brigade, which was holding the line north of the railway, was not involved in the attack, apart from a diversion and pro-viding one of its battalions as divisional reserve. Whitehead's 26th Brigade was allotted the northern half-mile of the final objective, after the capture of which it was to protect the north flank and exploit in that direction. The 'Red' line objectives were captured by 2/24th battalion soon after midnight. Little opposition had been met, they had had few casualties and were in touch with 2/17th battalion of 20th

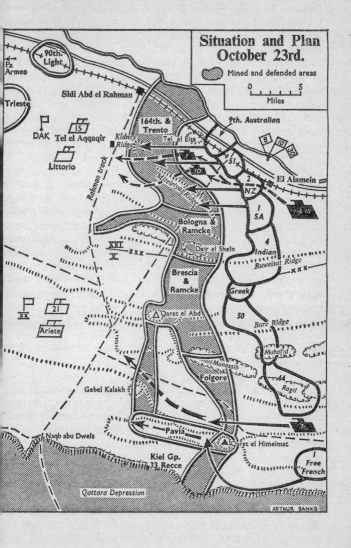

Situation and Plan October 23rd.

Mined and defended areas

0   5
Miles

Pz Armes

90th. Light

Sidi Abd el Rahman

Trieste

DAK

15

Tel el Aqqaqir

Littorio

Rahman track

164th. & Trento

Kidney Ridge

Tel el Eisa

9th. Australian

8   10   30

51

70

El Alamein

Miteiriya Ridge

2 NZ

1 & 10

Bologna & Ramcke

SA

Deir el Shein

4 Indian

Ruweisat Ridge

XXI X   XXX

Greek

50

Brescia & Ramcke

Bare Ridge

△ Qaret el Abd

XX   21

Ariete

Muhafid

Munassib

Folgore

44 Ragil

Gebel Kalakh

Naqb abu Dweis

Pavia

Kiel Gp. 33 Recce

Qaret el Himeimat

1 Free French

Qattara Depression

ARTHUR BANKS

Brigade on their left. 2/48th battalion passed through then
punctually at five to one and had captured their final object
ives on time at a quarter to three, having had stiff fighting
in the final stages.

There was not enough artillery to fire a barrage in fron
of the infantry: a programme of timed concentrations wa
therefore fired, most of it on the front of Wrigley's 20th
Brigade on the left. The brigade advanced to 'Red' line
with 2/17th battalion on the right and 2/15th on the left
Both reached their objectives on time at midnight with few
casualties, having met little opposition. 2/13th battalion wa
then to pass through with 40th Royal Tank Regiment, but
the tanks were delayed as enemy mines had not all been
cleared. The infantry colonel preferred to follow the artillery
programme rather than wait for the tanks and so set of
without them. He soon ran into strong opposition which
caused many casualties and brought the battalion to a halt
It was not till five in the morning that the tanks finally
got through and the advance was resumed. They were still
1,000 yards short of their final objective when dawn began
to break. The infantry hastily dug in while the tanks stayed
with them, withdrawing half a mile at half past seven to
less exposed positions. The brigade captured 127 German
from 164th Division and 264 Italians from Trento. Enemy
artillery fire had been light and opposition weak except
against the 2/13th. It had been a most satisfactory attack for
the whole division.

On their left Wimberley's Highlanders had a much more
difficult task in every way. Their final objectives covered a
front double the width of their start line and included many
of the strongest parts of the main defences. Their attack
led straight towards the area in which the enemy's northern
armoured divisions normally were, and they themselves had
to provide for the passage of 1st Armoured Division through
their front. Their plan was a more complicated one and to
make it intelligible they had introduced two intermediate
phase lines: 'Green' between the start line and 'Red', and
'Black' between 'Red' and the final 'Blue'. In addition
every known enemy defensive position was given the nam

of some prominent Scottish landmark, a town or a mountain. Every man had received Wimberley's special order of the day: 'As being in the proud position of Commander of the Highland Division of Scotland, I know that I am expressing for us all what every Scotsman feels in his heart today: "Scotland for ever and second to none".' For the benefit of the large number of Englishmen in the division he tactfully added: 'Special message for our diehards – "For ever England".' Each man carried his personal weapon and equipment, small pack with cardigan, bonnet or cap-comforter, two grenades, fifty rounds of extra ammunition in a bandolier, one day's rations and a full water-bottle. In addition white St Andrew's crosses of scrim were tied across the back of the small pack, in order to help the men following behind keep in touch with those in front in the dark. All were equipped with a pick or shovel and an entrenching tool. The former was fastened to the back of the small pack, to which four sandbags were tied. In the pack were a ground-sheet, shaving kit and iron ration. Thus each man was rationed and equipped to fight for at least twenty-four hours and, even if the ground were too hard for digging, he had four sandbags which he could fill to give himself some protection from shell-fire.

Murray's 152nd Brigade had been given the task of holding the front line, marking the start line and clearing and marking the routes forward to it. 5th Seaforth had done this on the two previous nights, while 5th Camerons had cleared eleven gaps in their own forward minefields at the western end of 'Sun', 'Moon' and 'Star' routes. Graham's 153rd Brigade was on the right, Houldsworth's 154th on the left. In the former, 5th Black Watch were to advance to 'Red' line where 1st Gordons would pass through to the final objective, 'Aberdeen'. On the left 5/7th Gordons would go all the way through from start to finish, the final stretch including 'Strichen'.

154th Brigade on the left had nearly three-quarters of the whole divisional front to cover. On the right 1st Black Watch with 7/10th Argyll and Sutherland Highlanders would go all the way through to their final objectives, which for both of them would include the strong enemy position 'Stirling'.

On the left of the brigade the attack to 'Red' line would be made by two companies of 5th Camerons, after which 7th Black Watch would pass through to link up with the New Zealanders at the extreme north-west end of Miteiriya Ridge. In between them and the Argylls, 50th Royal Tanks was to make its way forward as fast as mine clearance would allow to join in the final attack on 'Blue' line by capturing 'Nairn'.

Every man had a hot meal at seven o'clock, glad to stretch his legs after the cramped, hot day hidden in a slit trench. It was with great confidence and no little emotion that the division moved forward to the start line under cover of the counter-battery bombardment. Soon after ten the skirl of pipes could be heard all down the line. Captain Grant Murray of 5th Seaforth, out with a patrol covering the start line, saw the attack forming up:

> The hands of my watch seemed to creep round as we lay listening and watching. To our front all was quiet apart from a Verey light or two and some machine-gun fire. As zero drew near I twisted round and looked back towards our own lines. Suddenly the whole horizon went pink and for a second or two there was still perfect silence, and then the noise of 8th Army's guns hit us in a solid wall of sound that made the whole earth shake. Through the din we made out other sounds – the whine of shells overhead, the clatter of the machine-guns . . . and eventually the pipes. Then we saw a sight that will live for ever in our memories – line upon line of steel-helmeted figures with rifles at the high port, bayonets catching in the moonlight, and over all the wailing of the pipes. . . . As they passed they gave us the thumbs-up sign, and we watched them plod on towards the enemy lines, which by this time were shrouded in smoke. Our final sight of them was just as they entered the smoke, with the enemy's defensive fire falling among them.

On the right of Graham's 153rd Brigade 5th Black Watch crossed the start line at ten to ten and, with pipes playing, passed straight through the first minefield, led compass in hand by Captain East. In one of the leading companies, held up by a wire entanglement, the barber had appropriately been entrusted with the wire-cutters: 'Get a bloody

move on, Jock, you're no' cuttin' hair now' was heard through
the din of battle. It was not long before these companies
met opposition and men began to fall, among them nineteen-
year-old Piper Duncan McIntyre, who played as he died.
The straight line, forging ahead in the moonlight, soon
became ragged, dust and smoke adding to the confusion
caused by enemy fire. As paces became shorter, calculations
of distance went astray and there seems no doubt that 5th
Black Watch were nearer 'Green' than 'Red' when they
stopped at half past eleven for 1st Gordons to pass through.

While the latter were arguing about whether they really
were on 'Red' line or not, concentrated artillery fire began
to land 300 yards ahead. Some said it was our own guns
firing on 'Kintore', but the gunners swore it was the enemy.
The Gordons' colonel decided to wait for it to slacken off and
started at twelve minutes past midnight, nine minutes late.
The leading companies went steadily through the curtain
of fire and did not have many casualties, but what happened
after that is obscure. 'A' company eventually reached 'Braemar', 1,000 yards beyond 'Kintore' near 'Black' line, having
had heavy casualties. There they were later joined by 'C',
but nobody knew for certain whether either of them had
captured 'Kintore' on the way: probably not. The two
companies stormed 'Braemar' together and captured all but
a small part of it. By that time they could only muster 60
men with 3 officers between them, and remained out of
touch with their battalion headquarters until ten o'clock next
morning, when a runner got through. 'D' company had been
sent on with 'A' squadron of 50th Royal Tanks to help
attack 'Kintore', and the tanks then went on alone to attack
'Aberdeen', but ran into mines on the way. The battalion
was finally reorganised just west of 'Red' line, ignorant of the
fate of 'A' and 'C' companies and uncertain whether 'Kintore'
had been captured or not.

1st Gordons were not therefore exactly gay when dawn
broke and their 5/7th battalion on their left was little better
off. They had started off well, but ran into heavy fire as they
approached 'Red' line. After 1,000 yards under heavy shelling
they were held up by machine-guns firing from 'Strichen' and
'Keith' and covering what appeared to be an extensive mine-

field. Trying to outflank it, one company ran straight into another minefield, also covered by fire, and was cut to pieces. The other could not move and dug in where it was, half a mile short of 'Black' line and a mile and a half from their final objective. In spite of its narrow front therefore Graham's brigade was little in advance of 'Red' line by dawn and the enemy's main defence line in its sector was more or less intact.

On the right of Houldsworth's brigade 1st Black Watch set off fast and kept very close to the barrage from which they had few casualties. They reached 'Red' line on time, but after that were delayed and met plenty of opposition, most of which was cleared by bayonet and grenade. They finished beyond their final objective, which seems to have been on 'Black' rather than on 'Blue' line, and had to come back to it. The left-hand company continued to advance to 'Perth', also on 'Black' line, through a field full of anti-personnel mines covered by machine-gun fire, but on arrival there was out of touch with battalion headquarters and only one officer was left on his feet.

7/10th Argylls next in the line had the same sort of experience. All went well as far as 'Red' line, although opposition was growing and fire more intense as they reached it. When they started off beyond it, fighting became fierce and confused; the two leading companies were reduced to 30 men each, one was lost and the fourth delayed by mines with 'C' squadron 50th Royal Tanks, who with them were to capture 'Stirling'. Long before this the colonel, Lorne Campbell, had decided to dig in where he was. When they did arrive, the area was swept by fire from 'Stirling' and a daylight attack was considered out of the question.

On the left of the brigade 'B' and 'C' companies of 5th Camerons had had little difficulty in reaching 'Red' line. When 7th Black Watch passed through, they met little opposition at first, but mortar and artillery fire gradually increased until six navigating officers had either been killed or wounded. When they paused on 'Black' line for half an hour, the colonel realised that the leading companies had had very heavy casualties. One, no more than a platoon in strength, was sent on with Captain Cathcart's 'D' company, the remainder digging in on 'Black' line. Cathcart fought his way forward over the crest of Miteiriya Ridge and at four o'clock captured 'Kircaldy'. Here, reduced to less than 50 men, one officer killed and the rest including himself wounded, he made contact with the New Zealanders on his left and was in fact the only part of the Highland Division to reach the final objective set for it. This contact with the 21st New Zealand battalion was not easily made. The platoon commanders, who should have finished up next to each other, had met before the battle and arranged 'Jock' and 'Kiwi' as passwords for recognition; but both were killed before they reached their objectives. So was a runner from the 'Kiwis' on his way to the 'Jocks'. Private Smith of the Black Watch saw this and, although shot in the shoulder himself, on his own initiative went and found the message, brought it in and then offered to take back the answer. Cathcart himself and two of his wounded officers remained at duty all through the following day. In this night's action 7th Black Watch lost 15 officers, 5 of them killed, and nearly 200 men of whom 65 were killed.

In the centre 50th Royal Tanks had spent a most frustrating night, starting when attempts to clear 'F' gap for them ran into one difficulty after another. Scorpions failed to turn up, there were no mine detectors and the sappers, reduced to trying to clear a gap through 150 yards of minefield with nothing but bayonet-prodding, had a number of casualties. 'C' squadron were told to find their way to the 7th Argylls, which as we have seen they eventually did. The gap was clear by half past two, but another field was found. It was an hour later before the tanks were through and ready to attack 'Nairn'. They started slowly and were at once met by anti-tank fire on the right, which seemed to come from 'Stirling'. After three tanks had been knocked out the squadron withdrew to 'Black' line.

The Highland Division had fought hard and had suffered a considerable number of casualties. There were countless examples of courage, some recognised in the many awards granted to the division for the night's operation and many, doubtless just as gallant, unrecorded; but, except on the extreme left, the attack had not dealt with and certainly not penetrated the enemy's main defence line. The division had succeeded in making gaps for its own use in the enemy's forward minefields by about one o'clock, but the delays and difficulties in advancing beyond 'Red' line and the failure to clear up important positions like 'Kintore', 'Stirling' and 'Strichen' had held up mine clearance for 1st Armoured Division and therefore the move forward of their tanks. The dust, smoke, mines and general confusion of the battlefield, made much worse by the fact that two divisions of two different corps were trying to clear minefield gaps and get their vehicles forward in the same restricted area, from which the enemy had not been fully evicted, produced a chaotic situation in which nobody knew where they really were themselves, let alone where friend or foe might be.

The task facing Freyberg was very similar to Wimberley's. The front was narrower, one and a half miles widening to three in the end; but he only had two infantry brigades to draw on. The method he chose was somewhat different, taking more account of the need to develop the fullest strength in the last stages. Kippenberger's 5th Brigade on the right and Gentry's 6th on the left were each to attack to 'Red' line with one battalion only. After a pause of an hour and fifty minutes there, the remaining two battalions of both brigades were to pass through, pausing for a quarter of an hour again on their way to the final objectives beyond Miteiriya Ridge. 28th Maori Battalion was to follow with two companies behind each brigade mopping up enemy posts which had been missed. The main task of Currie's 8th Armoured Brigade with the divisional cavalry was to pass through the infantry at the final objective and take up positions in front of them in order both to deal with counter-attacks and also to exploit success to the south. During the night attack the Royal Wiltshire Yeomanry, with 14 Grants, 10 Shermans and 13 Crusaders, were to support 5th Brigade and the Warwickshire Yeomanry, with 3 more Shermans and 4 more Crusaders, the 6th. The other regiment, 3rd Hussars, had 9 Grants, 12 Shermans and 16 Crusaders. The use of the tanks would depend on the speed at which the divisional engineers cleared gaps for the two routes forward on each brigade front.

The divisional artillery, reinforced by six troops from 10th Corps, fired a timed programme of concentrations on known defences, one regiment only firing a very thin barrage across the whole front mainly to help the infantry to keep direction. In 5th Brigade the 23rd battalion met considerable mortar and shell fire just short of the first enemy minefield, but had crossed it in the first half-hour with few casualties. They got beyond their 'Red' line objective and met strong opposition, suffering heavy casualties before they came back to it; but the Maoris coming up behind helped them out. The 23rd lost in all 129 men and had not got back to their proper place when the 21st arrived there.

The latter started the second phase on time at five minutes to one with three companies abreast. They reached their final objectives punctually at a quarter to three, having had a number of casualties from mortaring and shelling. There they dug in on the forward slopes of the ridge, while contact was made with 7th Black Watch on the right and the reserve company sent forward to attack enemy guns. Trouble at the minefield gaps delayed the arrival of their anti-tank guns, machine-guns and mortars.

The left battalion of the brigade, the 22nd, had a more difficult time. The enemy post, which had caused trouble to the 23rd when they went beyond their objective, held them up for some time, but was later attacked from the flank and wiped out. Little further opposition was met and soon after half past two all three leading companies were on their objectives, although subjected to heavy mortar fire. Patrols then went forward and returned with over 60 prisoners, bringing the battalion's bag to 150 to offset their own casualties of 110.

By half past four Kippenberger was well established west of Miteiriya Ridge. There had been delays in clearing routes forward, work on the first minefield not having started until a quarter past midnight. By half past one the northern gap had been reported clear, after two Scorpions had broken down. The engineers started on the second minefield at five to four and only cleared a way through by half past five. By that time a further field on the top of Miteiriya Ridge had been found, which the Maoris helped to clear before they were withdrawn at half past six. It was therefore not until just before it was light that there was a route clear up to the ridge.

24th battalion led Gentry's attack on the left with three companies in line. They soon began to suffer from machine-gun fire from the left where the South Africans were held up. As a result they veered off to the right and came under more heavy fire when they reached the first minefield. One company then went off to the left to deal with this while the others went on. The battalion had 10 killed and 77 wounded by the time they reached 'Red' line.

26th battalion, following them up on the right, had been delayed and went straight through without ever seeing the 24th. Soon afterwards they ran into heavy shelling, uncertain whether it was fired by our own artillery or by the enemy. They were under intense machine-gun fire from the left, but by dawn were established on the forward slope of Miteiriya Ridge without their supporting weapons, but in touch with the 22nd on the right and the 25th on the left.

Like the 26th, the 25th had missed the 24th on 'Red' line. They met considerable opposition after that, and by dawn their forward companies were only just on and short of the ridge, prevented from getting forward beyond it by enemy posts on either flank. On their right they were in touch with the 26th, but there was a 400-yard gap between them. There was no sign of the South Africans on their left. Their supporting weapons arrived only as dawn was breaking and, like those of the 26th, were hastily deployed east of the ridge. The two Maori companies mopping up behind 6th Brigade could find none of the forward battalions, but went cheerfully forward on their own until they reached the ridge, where they took up their positions on either flank of the 25th, one company on the left having had to attack and capture an enemy post on the way.

Currie's tanks had a slow and dusty move forward, as it was three o'clock before they began to move through the first minefield. On the right the Wiltshire Yeomanry reached the crest of the ridge just as dawn broke, but their heavy squadrons then ran on to a minefield, losing 9 tanks. The remaining 15 continued on and were at once engaged by 30 to 40 enemy tanks, in face of which they withdrew behind the ridge and refuelled. On their left the Warwickshire Yeomanry had reached the eastern slope of the ridge by four o'clock. In attempting to move forward the leading squadron lost 6 tanks on mines, and the rest took up positions just before dawn on the right of the 25th and behind 26th battalion. 3rd Hussars were in reserve behind 24th battalion when they were heavily shelled at half past six. They dispersed and later moved on to the ridge on the right of the Warwickshires behind 22nd battalion.

By dawn therefore the New Zealand division had reached its objective beyond the ridge, except on the left where they rested on it. The delay in clearing minefield gaps meant that most of the forward companies had not got the weapons they needed to make them secure against attack. The unexpected minefield on the ridge itself and then the opposition beyond had prevented Currie's tanks from getting forward. There was however a route clear of mines right through Kippenberger's sector. As there was no sign of Gatehouse passing through, there was no question for the moment of 'exploiting to the south-west', even if the division had been capable of doing so, which is doubtful.

Pienaar's task and the method he chose to execute it were both very much the same as Freyberg's. 2nd Brigade on the right and 3rd on the left were each to use one battalion for the first phase up to 'Red' line. After a pause of an hour and a quarter, the other two battalions were to pass through to the final objectives beyond Miteiriya Ridge. 1st Brigade was to find a special force of armoured cars, machine-guns and anti-tank guns to guard the left flank, and a mobile reserve of 8th Royal Tanks and 2nd Regiment Botha was to advance in the centre and help to capture the final objective, meet counter-attacks and exploit southwards thereafter. The divisional artillery, reinforced by three field troops from 10th Corps and a medium battery, was to fire a programme of timed concentrations, also using smoke on the intermediate and final objectives to cover reorganisation and to help with direction-finding.

1st Natal Mounted Rifles captured 'Red' line in 2nd Brigade's sector without difficulty. Cape Town Highlanders, due to pass through on the right, got involved in serious and confused fighting on their start line and suffered considerable casualties, including the two leading company commanders. This led to the artillery programme for the second phase being postponed several times, while attempts were made to deal with the opposition and sort out the confusion. Although it started again at five minutes past two, it was not till half past four that the infantry advance was resumed. It then met no serious opposition and the battalion was established on Miteiriya Ridge by first light. On the left 1st/2nd Field Force Battalion also ran into trouble, including an unexpected minefield. After some difficult and confused fighting the battalion established itself just east of the ridge, a mile short of their final objective, having had 42 men killed, 8 officers and 133 men wounded and having captured 36 Germans.

1st Rand Light Infantry, leading 3rd Brigade, came up against a strong enemy position only a quarter of an hour after crossing the start line. With the help of Bangalore torpedoes they captured it, took some prisoners from the German 164th division and pushed on to 'Red' line, which they reached by ten minutes to midnight. They continued to have trouble with the right flank, not helped by the delay in 2nd Brigade, and had about 100 casualties, including 10 officers.

The postponement of the artillery programme for the second phase helped the Imperial Light Horse on the left, as they had been delayed by the Rand Light Infantry's difficulties. Neither they nor the Royal Durban Light Infantry had much difficulty in getting forward after that, although the right flank of the latter was troublesome. Both battalions were on their objectives by five o'clock, the Light Infantry having had about 50 casualties and the Light Horse only 9.

The divisional reserve group spent a typically frustrating night owing to delays and difficulties over clearing minefield gaps. It was daylight before they reached the eastern slopes of Miteiriya Ridge behind the Royal Durban Light Infantry. The Transvaal Scottish and the machine-gunners of the

Regiment President Steyn came up on the left flank without
difficulty or casualties.

By dawn therefore the division, having suffered about
350 casualties, was on its objectives except on the right, but
in no position to exploit southwards, as foreseen. Further
south 4th Indian Division had successfully carried out the
raids and diversions allotted to it.

If 30th Corps felt that their part in the battle had so far
been fairly satisfactorily achieved, the same could not be
said of 10th Corps, which had spent a most trying and
frustrating night. Its tank strength on the evening of the
23rd stood at 434: 161 in Fisher's 2nd Armoured Brigade
(one Grant, 92 Shermans and 68 Crusaders), 133 in Custance's 8th (2 Grants, 93 Shermans and 45 Crusaders) and
140 in Kenchington's 24th (57 Grants, 31 Shermans and 45
Crusaders). Briggs' 1st Armoured Division was to pass
through near the boundary between the Australians and the
Highland Division, while Gatehouse's 10th did the same on
the New Zealander's front. 30th Corps had no responsibility
for clearing gaps in enemy minefields for the armour and
each armoured division had therefore to form a minefield task
force of its own. This force had to make at least three gaps
for its division in all enemy minefields, marking them and
the routes forward from the exits of our own forward minefield, and working in close co-operation with the infantry
division attacking on its front. The task force was composed
of a motor battalion, three engineer field squadrons and
three troops of Crusader tanks: signals and military police
were also included. In 1st Armoured Division it was under
the commanding officer of the motor battalion, but in the
10th under the Commander Royal Engineers. The divisions
were to leave their assembly areas near El Imayid station after
dark, the leading vehicles reaching the track running south
from El Alamein, called Springbok Road, at half past midnight. They were to start forward from there, having refuelled, at two o'clock unless Montgomery ordered otherwise,
each division on three tracks only 500 yards apart; the 1st on
Sun, Moon and Star; the 10th on Bottle, Boat and Hat.

It was hoped that the leading tanks of Fisher's and Custance's brigades would debouch from 30th Corps' final

objectives well before dawn. As they moved forward to the
first bound, called 'Pierson', about three miles to the west,
Kenchington would come up on the left of Custance and the
tanks of the whole Corps would then be in a position to
meet an enemy attack. In the next stage, which was unlikely
to be before it was light, Fisher on the right and Kenchington on the left would advance for another mile, while Bosvile's riflemen emerged as flank guard on the north and Lee's
lorried infantry on the south. The final stage, which would
certainly be in daylight, would bring Fisher south-west a
further two miles to the Rahman track, while Custance
moved into position just south of it after a westward advance
of four miles. While this was going on and as soon as it was
light, armoured cars were to make their way forward 10
miles to the north-west to try and locate 15th Panzer Division
and also south towards Deir el Shein to give warning of any
northward move of the southern armoured group.

The Corps had absolute priority on all tracks after two
o'clock in the morning. There were no illusions as to how
vague and confused the situation might be. It was accepted
that the brigades might have to deploy into battle formation
from their line-ahead columns at any time and that they
might themselves have to force the final break-out. It was
hoped that one or more of the brigades would be able to
envelop the flank of the enemy's tanks while the third, probably Fisher's, met them head-on. By this means it was expected that the northern group of armour would be destroyed
before the southern group could join it. Lumsden's final word
of warning had been: 'On no account to rush blindly on to
enemy anti-tank guns or try to pass through a narrow bottleneck covered by a concentration of tanks. In such cases a
proper co-ordinated plan was to be made. anti-tank guns
being engaged by artillery and machine-guns.'

Briggs' minefield task force was delayed by a last-minute
decision to allow the New Zealanders to use Star track from
seven o'clock until three in the morning, but on all three
tracks the gapping parties were at work by twenty past
midnight. They immediately ran into great difficulties. On
Sun route there were few mines in the first field and a 16-

yard-wide gap was through before one o'clock. After that a great many scattered groups of mines were met, but there was a gap through the second field by two. Three hours later the third minefield was also gapped and there was a clear route through to as far as the infantry had reached.

The parties on the other routes were not so lucky or successful. On Moon track the first field had to be cleared by bayonet prodding as the detectors did not work, and a 16-yard gap was not finished until ten past four. Further progress was prevented by the enemy post at 'Kintore', which 1st Gordons did not finally clear up until nearly nine in the morning. A gap in the second minefield was then cleared, but it was impossible to go on to the third. On 'Star' route lifting was slow. The allotment of the route further back to the New Zealanders and a last-minute change in the officer in charge contributed to this. It was not till two that the first minefield was gapped and by half past four there was still only an 8-yard gap in the second. Even this could not be used owing to the enemy position at 'Strichen' which 5/7th Gordons had not cleared.

In spite of this lack of gaps Fisher's tanks moved forward slowly as planned, the Bays group on Sun track on the right, 9th Lancers group and brigade headquarters on Moon in the centre, and 10th Hussars group on Star, heads of columns reaching the first enemy minefield soon after four. Three Shermans were disabled on scattered mines and there was a good deal of doubt and argument about where everybody was. By this time the whole area was enveloped in dust, there were masses of vehicles all over the place and the marking of the routes and gaps was very hard to see. It needed only a vehicle or two to stray off the side to remove all the signs and lead everybody behind into confusion. Tempers got as heated as the engines while the tanks and other vehicles ground along at snail's pace in the billowing clouds of dust.

At five the Bays reported themselves nearing the third minefield, but an hour later, just as it was getting light, they were held up immediately behind the forward infantry. When it was light, they said they were through the last enemy minefield and were engaging enemy anti-tank guns with both heavy squadrons deployed. In fact they were only just

west of the first minefield, short of 'Red' line and three or
four miles east of where they thought; but this was not
realised until at least an hour later and their exact position
continued to be a bone of contention for several days.

9th Lancers on Moon were held up by the failure to
clear gaps. They only started to pass through the first minefield at dawn and deployed on both sides of it, while their
motor company, 'B' squadron of the Yorkshire Dragoons,
went forward to try and help clear up 'Kintore'. On Star
10th Hussars were in the same position, unable to use the
narrow gap in the second minefield because of fire from
'Strichen', and at dawn they deployed in an area thick with
mines. Although there had been little enemy artillery fire and
the brigade had had very few casualties, it was still east of
the enemy's minefields when day broke.

Gatehouse's minefield-clearing plans had been based on the
assumption that there were only two fields to gap. On Bottle
route the first was clear by two o'clock, and by half past four
there was a clear route marked right up to Miteiriya Ridge.
On Ink route there was more delay due to enemy opposition,
but a route forward to the ridge was clear by a quarter past
five, by which time Boat was also through in spite of similar
difficulties. The clearing parties on Hat had the hardest time
of all, but, after having had to deal with both enemy opposition and many more mines than expected, they were re-
warded by finding a gap ready made by the enemy in the
second field. By dawn therefore there were four routes clear
to Miteiriya Ridge, but only Boat was actually in use at the
western end.

With two armoured brigades Gatehouse had a lot more
traffic to cope with than Briggs. Custance's brigade led with
the Staffordshire Yeomanry group on Bottle track on the
right, the Nottinghamshire Yeomanry (Sherwood Rangers)
group on Boat in the centre and 3rd Royal Tanks group
on Hat on the left, followed by the armoured cars of the
Royals. Divisional headquarters followed in the centre and
then Kenchington's brigade with 41st Royal Tanks group on
Bottle, the 47th on Boat and the 45th on Hat. Finally
Lee's brigade had to grope along at the back with its three

battalions of the Royal Sussex, the 5th on the right, 4th in the centre and 2nd on the left.

The Staffordshire made good progress on Bottle, and at half past five were approaching the crest of Miteiriya Ridge when they found another minefield there which enemy anti-tank guns prevented them from crossing. They took up hull-down positions on the reverse slope of the ridge, where they found themselves immediately on the left of their old comrades in arms of 1st Cavalry Division, the Warwickshire Yeomanry of Currie's brigade.

When the Sherwood Rangers on Boat track crossed the ridge after passing through the second minefield soon after five, their leading Crusader squadron came under intense anti-tank gun fire at close range. The heavy squadrons behind deployed to right and left, firing smoke to cover their with-drawal. Both squadrons, and 'B' battery 1st Royal Horse Artillery who had followed them, were then brought back behind the crest as the light improved, but not until eight Crusaders and the same number of Grants had been lost.

3rd Royal Tanks had been much delayed by the difficulties in clearing minefield gaps on Hat route. They did not begin to pass through the first minefield until half past four and as dawn broke were still laboriously working their way through. They were ordered to disperse as best they could and finally came into position on the ridge to the left of the Sherwood Rangers. As might be expected, the Royals had no success in trying to get out on the flanks, losing one car on a mine on the right and two knocked out by 88-mm. guns on the left. Divisional headquarters had stopped where Boat track crossed Springbok road three miles south-west of El Alamein station, Lee's brigade being dispersed in the same area.

Kenchington's brigade and the Royals had to find room for themselves in the old no-man's-land, already overcrowded with artillery and vehicles of the New Zealand and South African Divisions, not to mention the tail of 8th Armoured Brigade. Dispersion, as far as it was possible at all, was a hazardous business, as mines were by no means confined to regular fields and slit trenches abounded. The congestion was appalling and the confusion considerable. The whole area looked like a badly organised car park at an immense race meeting held in a dust bowl.

Down in the south Harding's 7th Armoured Division, the only formation of 13th Corps to be actively engaged, had been experiencing much the same difficulties as beset both 30th and 10th Corps. However they had the advantage that the whole operation of trying to force a way through the enemy's defences just north of Himeimat was theirs alone: there were none of the difficulties of divided command and responsibility that arose in the north.

Horrocks' plan covered three phases. In the first Harding, supported by Hughes' artillery and one corps field regiment in addition to his own, was to penetrate January and February minefields between Munassib and Himeimat, while Koenig's 1st Free French Brigade, under Harding's command, was to capture the area immediately west of Himeimat itself. Hughes was then to take over the defence of the bridgehead west of the minefield gaps. In the second phase Harding was to clear up the opposition as far west as Gebel Kalakh and the Taqa plateau, while 50th Division straightened out the front between themselves and the 44th. Finally the Corps was to be prepared to penetrate beyond the area of Qaret el Abd and Gebel Kalakh.

Apart from artillery support, the only part which 44th Division had to play in the initial attack was for 1/7th Queen's of 131st Brigade to establish themselves between January and February to protect Roberts' right flank. Unfortunately things went wrong at an early stage, and the battalion suffered heavy casualties, including their colonel who was killed after gallantly leading the remnants on himself. They were rallied by the adjutant just east of January, the sappers bravely gapping the field west of them on their own.

7th Armoured Division had a long approach march of nearly 10 miles on four parallel routes through three of their own minefields to reach the start line, just east of January. Their minefield task force was formed by 44th Divisional Reconnaissance Regiment, which had absorbed the carrier platoons of the division and also 4th Field Squadron Royal Engineers. It was supported by six Scorpions, 'A' squadron of the Greys, an anti-tank battery and two companies of

1st/60th. Their job was to clear and mark four gaps in both January and February minefields.

22nd Armoured Brigade set off at a quarter to seven from May minefield, and all went well in the brilliant moonlight in spite of occasional patches of soft sand. Roberts halted the cavalcade at eight o'clock for thirty-five minutes, as they were ahead of time and he did not want to arrive at the start line too early and have to hang about there. Unfortunately, when they started off again, many of the lamps marking the route had gone out and there was much delay, with the result that the gapping parties were twenty-five minutes late at the start line. This and some shelling meant that forming up was a hurried affair and the advance to January was ten minutes behind programme.

After a number of mistakes and difficulties, number one gap in the north was finally cleared by half past four, although there was an enemy post just west of the exit. In number two gap the Scorpion was disabled by a mine and anti-tank gun fire, but the gap was cleared by hand at twenty to two. The squadron responsible for numbers three and four gaps hit mines in a deep sandy wadi soon after crossing the start line. They thought it must be the east edge of January, which it was not, and started their Scorpion flailing. It broke down repeatedly from overheating, there was a lot of enemy fire of all kinds, progress was slow and there had been many casualties before even the eastern edge of January was reached. By that time however the magnificent efforts of the crews had got all Scorpions working again. Number three gap was eventually through by a quarter past two, although it was of no use to wheeled vehicles owing to the soft sand, and one of the Scorpions was disabled at the western end. The Scorpion in number four gap was knocked out when it was three-quarters of the way through, but the gap was finished by hand as early as half past midnight.

The first troops through the gaps in January were 1st Rifle Brigade, 'A' company on the two northern routes, 'B' on the southern. The latter were in great difficulties both with the soft sand and with enemy fire from the south. This slackened a bit when 'A' turned south to help, followed by a squadron of the Greys. Roberts sent 5th Royal Tanks through the two northern gaps to come up on the right of the Greys, and they were through an hour later; but on the southern routes 1st Royal Tanks were still kept east of January waiting for the Rifle Brigade to get on.

Soon after the barrage had started [wrote Lieutenant Peter Luke of the Rifle Brigade] my truck had got stuck in some soft sand at the entrance to the gap in the minefield, thus isolating those who had gone before and blocking effectively the main armoured force to follow. A carrier-load of the first wounded – a pretty gory lot, one fellow with his leg off at the thigh and another lying on his stomach with his back ripped up – was also trying to get back through the narrow gap. If physical strength had been equal to our endeavour we would have lifted our vehicle bodily out on to the hard bit of ground only a few yards away but, though desperation had given me maniacal strength, there was nothing we could do owing to the weight of the extra machine-gun ammunition we were carrying. We had just begun to unload the truck when one of our guns taking part in the barrage started to drop them short; thenceforward for the next quarter of an hour it plopped a 25-pound shell at short regular intervals into our vicinity.

We had set out on the approach march in high spirits. I was certainly greatly elated and communicated it, I think, to the others. At the opening of the spectacular barrage Sergeant Jefford said, 'I'll bet that's making Old Jerry **** blue lights!' and we all roared. And when this gunner behind us began laying short the men still joked, slightly hysterically, with such remarks as, 'I'll tell 'is muvver abaht 'im' and so on.

Just as we had all the ammunition on the ground, one landed within 10 yards of the truck. Because it landed in the same patch of soft sand that we were stuck in, most of the shrapnel went upwards; but it was sobering and at that stage we had not properly joined the battle.

At that moment Hugh, my company commander, appeared on foot from the gap where he had been with the leading platoon. 'What in God's name are you doing?'

he said without – quite understandably – giving a thought
to the convention of not bawling at an officer in front of
his troops. 'You're holding up a whole armoured division.'

In spite of the cool night the sweat was pouring down
my face and I think this concealed the tears of frustration
that came to my eyes. Also my shortness of breath from
exertion concealed the catch in my voice when I said, 'I'm
sorry, Hugh, but I couldn't avoid the soft sand. There
wasn't room'.

'I don't care. Get that bloody vehicle out of here and
get up forward where you're wanted.'

His tone, it seemed to me then, implied that I had deliberately got myself stuck in order to avoid going on. In
fact, at that moment, though never thereafter, I would
have rushed alone on to a Panzer Grenadier regiment. It
seemed that the Scorpion had been knocked out by an
anti-tank gun and that my Vickers machine-guns were required to put this last out of action. Abandoning my truck
to the crew I ran forward through the soft sand and the
narrow lane the Scorpion had ploughed until I was blowing
like a tubed race-horse. The few seconds saved by this
exertion would not, of course, have made the slightest
difference to the outcome of the battle but I was stung by
Hugh's apparent unfairness.

Hugh was standing by the black and uncomfortably
conspicuous monument of the dead Scorpion with my leading machine-gun truck behind it. A platoon on foot with
some sappers was vaguely weaving about in front; beyond
them was the enemy, dug-in and invisible except for
irregular streams of tracer-bullets that seemed to come
very slowly out of the ground like the unfolding of a
Japanese paper water-plant.

Hugh pointed out the muzzle-flash of the anti-tank gun
as it fired again and almost instantaneously something like
a very fast ball on a dry wicket bumped on the ground
near the tank and bounced off into the air in a whirring
long-hop.

'Get on to that bloody gun before they hit the Scorpion's
petrol tank and light up the whole gap.'

'Okay, Hugh,' I said, confidence restored with the prospect of making myself, at last, effective. Jumping on to the truck next to Halsey, the driver, I told him to pull off to the left and go about a hundred yards away from the Scorpion. Hugh, in a less peremptory tone of voice, said something about manhandling the machine-gun because of the possibility of more mines but, because of the pandemonium of gun-fire, I waved ambiguous acknowledgement and set off with nothing now in front but the moon and the occasional flash from our objective, cheerful at the prospect of vindicating myself.

The next thing seemed to be a great concussion that occurred almost simultaneously with my biting, literally, the dust. It so winded me that for a moment I could not breathe. In this condition I realised that we had gone over a mine. . . .

By now the minefield task force had been greatly reduced by casualties, and its colonel, Corbett-Winder, told Roberts that he had only enough men to make two gaps in February. This was agreed and 'Y' hour for the start of the attack on February was fixed for half past five. On the right they never reached it: on the left they got there and came under heavy fire. As dawn was breaking and it was obviously impossible to clear the minefield gaps in daylight, they were withdrawn, one Scorpion being hit and having to be abandoned in full view of the enemy.

When daylight came the brigade was very congested on both sides of January. It was an uncomfortable and exposed position, particularly as the Free French were soon to be driven off the position they had reached just west of Himeimat. Their attack was carried out by 'Group A', consisting of the 1st and 2nd Foreign Legion battalions under Colonel Amilakvari. After a long and difficult approach march through very soft going, intersected by many wadis, these two battalions had reached their forming-up areas inside the enemy's minefield just south-west of Himeimat at half past one. The attack, launched north-eastwards an hour later, was supported by their own artillery and helped by a smoke-screen laid by the RAF. The 1st battalion on the right met strong opposition. Shortly before dawn Amilakvari told

Winston Churchill visiting Eighth Army Headquarters, August, 1942: with (left) Lieut.-General Alexander and Lieut.-General Montgomery

Montgomery with Lieut.-General von Thoma, Commander of the German Afrika Korps, after von Thoma's capture, 4 November 1942

Field Marshall Erwin Rommel, (second from the right) confers with his staff

The German army on the battlefield near Tobruk

Sappers of the Highland Division defusing mines

Members of the regiment of Gurkhas which fought at El Alamein

Australian troops attacking under cover of a smokescreen

A British Crusader tank passes a blazing German tank

the 2nd battalion on the left to attack, and they reached the northern edge of the escarpment half an hour later. By this time it was getting light and it had not been found possible to get any anti-tank guns up to them. At half past seven they were attacked by the eight captured Stuart tanks of the German Kiel group, who managed to evade the Crusaders of the Free French Flying Column. The 2nd battalion was forced to withdraw and, in so doing, exposed the rear of the 1st, who had to conform. Koenig gave Amilakvari permission to pull back about three miles to the south-east; but the withdrawal on foot in daylight across the bare slopes led to considerable loss of men. Amilakvari himself was killed and all their vehicles were lost. The death of their inspiring and popular commander was a severe blow to the Foreign Legion's morale, and the whole operation collapsed. The situation was not fully realised until considerably later.

At a quarter to eight Horrocks had told de Guingand that he would discuss with Harding 'whether to punch a hole through February or not'. If not, he proposed to 'crumble' between January and February.

8 THRASHING AROUND

October 24th – 25th

All that Stumme and his acting Chief of Staff, Westphal, knew for a long time was that an artillery bombardment on a scale unheard of since 1918 had opened along almost the entire length of the front and soon smashed their whole communication network, with the result that nobody knew what was happening. Stumme, anxious about his supply of ammunition, did not authorise immediate retaliation. It was said by his staff, and repeated by Rommel, that this was a grave error in that the British could not be shelled in their assembly positions. When the German artillery did eventually open fire, its effect was greatly reduced, it is said, because by that time the British had been able to install themselves in the German defences which they captured. There is little to support this. The inactivity of the German artillery in the earlier stages was clearly due as much to the counter-battery programme as to anything else. The guns were sited well back and few of them could reach areas in which the infantry would have been sufficiently concentrated to form a very vulnerable target. There is in fact very little evidence to show that the German or Italian artillery deliberately held their fire at any stage nor that the British infantry gained much from the use of the enemy's old defences. Rommel admitted that 8th Army's artillery fire was 'extra-ordinarily accurate', that 'enormous casualties' resulted, and that it destroyed most of the infantry's heavy weapons. So fierce was it that part of the Italian 62nd Infantry Regiment of Trento division is said to have left its positions and streamed to the rear, probably on the front of the Australians, which would account for the weakness of the opposition there. The impression at Panzer Armee headquarters was that the British had brought up tanks 'again and again', and had destroyed the remnants of 62nd Infantry Regiment and at least two battalions of 164th division. In the north it was believed that they had broken into the main defence line on a front of six miles, but had been stopped by concentrated artillery fire. In the south an attack had been launched with about 100 tanks which had overrun the outposts, but had been stopped in front of the main defence line.

As the situation was so obscure, Stumme decided to go and find out for himself what had happened. He was accompanied only by Colonel Buechting and his driver, Corporal Wolf, and refused to take an escort vehicle and a wireless truck on the grounds that he was only going as far as 90th Light Division. In fact he went right up to the front and was fired on, probably by the Australians. Buechting received a mortal wound in the head, and Wolf turned the car round and drove off at full speed. Stumme had been on the point of jumping out and seems to have hung on to the outside, had a heart attack and fallen off. He was known to be suffering from high blood pressure and was not really fit. It was not until Wolf slowed up that he realised what had happened, and the body was not found for twenty-four hours. This incident did not encourage decisive counter-action by the Panzer Armee at this critical period of the battle.

The picture was clearer at Montgomery's headquarters, but the exact position in the crucial sectors, where Briggs and Gatehouse had been intended to break through, was far from accurately known and the general outlook was undoubtedly optimistic. It was obvious that neither Lumsden in the north nor Harding in the south had broken through; but in the north at least this was thought to be largely due to the fact that there were still mines to be cleared before they could get going. At a quarter past nine, an hour before Alexander was due to arrive at his headquarters, Montgomery ordered Leese to give first priority to clearing 'the northern lane'. Freyberg was to exploit his success to the south, and Wimberley would then take over his sector of the ridge; but this would not be before the afternoon. Morshead was not to exploit the north, but was to be prepared to start a 'crumbling' operation that night.

Shortly after seven in the morning Freyberg had told Leese that he thought the moment had come for 'a supreme effort by 10th Armoured Division to pass through'. He thought that everything was set for Custance and Kenchington to reinforce Currie's battered brigade and force their way clear of the enemy's defences, as had been planned. Three-quarters of an hour later he was on the telephone again, asking Leese to urge Lumsden to hurry Gatehouse forward. This was done and Lumsden replied that the slow progress was due to the congestion of New Zealand division traffic in the only mine-free lane on their sector. Every effort would however be made to get them forward. As nothing more happened in the next two hours, the New Zealand Chief of Staff told 30th Corps at half past ten that Currie had been ordered to push on immediately. As he would be considerably out-numbered, Gatehouse should be ordered to push through to support him. 10th Corps replied that the division could not do it and that Lumsden considered that it was 'not on'. 30th Corps told the New Zealanders that Leese was on his way to see Freyberg and would sort it out on his arrival. It is not clear whether Currie was in fact given any such order. His brigade spent the day engaging enemy tanks from the shelter of the ridge, any attempt to cross which was immediately met with heavy and accurate anti-tank gun fire. By mid-day the Wiltshire Yeomanry had only one Sherman and three Grants left, and eight officers, including their colonel, Sykes, had been wounded.

Leese and Freyberg visited the ridge together, satisfying themselves that it was at least secure against counter-attack before they returned to the New Zealand headquarters to meet Montgomery and Lumsden. By now a more realistic view of the situation prevailed, and at mid-day it was de-cided that Gatehouse should attack that night through the New Zealanders, supported by the full weight of Leese's artillery. In case of any doubt about his intention, Mont-gomery on his return to his headquarters telephoned to Peake, Lumsden's Chief of Staff, and told him that another effort to get through the bridgehead must be made, and that he was prepared to accept casualties to ensure that the ar-moured divisions got out and the New Zealanders got on with their southward exploitation. De Guingand was now able to tell him that there was no sign of either 21st Panzer or 90th Light Division having moved: 1,000 prisoners two-thirds of them Italian, had been captured. 8th Army's own casualties were not accurately known, but probably came to less than 3,000 of which the great majority were in 30th Corps, the Highland Division having had about 1,000 and the New Zealanders about 800. The Australians and the South Africans had each lost about 350 men.

Meanwhile Wimberley was trying to 'clear the northern lane' by attacking 'Strichen' and 'Keith' with 2nd Seaforth who had been in reserve, supported by 50th Royal Tanks and the whole divisional artillery. Arguments were ceaseless about where everybody was, particularly between the division and 1st Armoured. An offer by the Commander of 30th Corps artillery to adjudicate was declined. The Seaforth had very little time in which to prepare for their attack, which was intended to make it possible for Briggs' engineers to clear the way for Fisher's tanks to advance immediately afterwards. The attack was launched at three o'clock and was successful in spite of heavy casualties in one company, which was finally rallied on the objective by the company clerk, all the officers and the sergeant-major having been killed or wounded.

The Bays on Fisher's right lost six Shermans from tank or anti-tank fire as soon as they had passed through the mine-field in front of them, probably the original second. They withdrew under smoke and were told to try a bit further south near 9th Lancers. The latter had met another mine-field as soon as they were clear of the one gapped in front of them. With sappers walking in front of the tanks they eventually joined up with the Bays, but there was still no sign of the 10th Hussars who were trying to get round a strong enemy position on the left. At five o'clock the two regiments went on together north-westwards, and by last light they were just north-east of Kidney Ridge. They withdrew 500 yards after dark, protected by the Yorkshire Dragoons, in the belief that they were on their objective, but in fact being 1,000 yards short of it. The brigade had lost 20 Shermans, 11 in the Bays, and was now at a strength of 57, having about the same number of Crusaders. They thought they had been up against about 80 enemy tanks of which they claimed to have knocked out 30, undoubtedly an optimistic estimate. That night Briggs decided to bring forward 7th Motor Brigade, still back near El Alamein station, to relieve the armour.

Further south Gatehouse had visited Miteiriya Ridge soon after first light and decided that it was not possible to send his tanks beyond it. An order at half past ten to send Kenchington up north to the east of the ridge, in order to attack the enemy holding up Fisher, had also been found impracticable because of mines. The plan for the night's break-out was for Currie to be withdrawn to make room for Kenchington, who would then attack southwestwards along the northern boundary of 10th Armoured Division's original break-through sector. Custance would attack to the south of them, and both brigades would advance three miles to 'Pierson' and link up with Fisher on the right. It was later decided that Currie would also attack on the left, Lee's lorried infantry replacing Custance's and Currie's tanks on the ridge. The divisional engineers were to clear as many 16-yard-wide gaps in the minefield on the ridge as they could.

It had not long been dark before Freyberg was on the telephone to Leese again, saying that he was by no means confident that 10th Armoured Division was 'properly set up for the attack' and remarking that the divisional headquarters was a long way back. Leese spoke to Lumsden and got the impression that the latter had little confidence in the success of the attack. These impressions were immediately passed on to de Guingand.

Kenchington started with 83 Shermans and 48 Crusaders, and his brigade was delayed from the start by confusion in the minefield gapping parties. Work did not start until a quarter to eleven, an hour after the gaps should have been clear. The field was deeper than expected and further delay was caused by a false report of an enemy attack which caused their commander to withdraw them, in the course of which they lost touch with their infantry escort. Finally all available resources were concentrated on making one gap, which was through by a quarter to four. Then the wireless to report it could not be found. Custance's sappers had no

time to find out about the minefield in which they were
to clear three, if possible four, 16-yard-wide gaps. They
started work at eight, and by half past ten the right and
centre gaps were through. The southern one was on the
line of a gap made by the enemy themselves: the exit was
covered by heavy fire and the attempt to clear it was
abandoned. The Staffordshire Yeomanry were on the right,
the Sherwood Rangers in the centre and 3rd Royal Tanks on
the left. As the area off the tracks was heavily mined, vehicles were packed nose to tail and double banked on each
route. At ten o'clock one, or perhaps two, aircraft came over-
head and a stick of bombs fell on the Sherwood Rangers as
they were waiting to go through the centre gap. A second
attack hit their transport and some of the vehicles of 1st
Buffs. Soon about 25 lorries carrying petrol and ammunition were on fire: the blaze continued all night, while the
enemy's artillery used it as a ranging point and went on
shelling the whole area. Four officers were wounded and the
Sherwood Rangers were disorganised for a time. Custance
ordered them to disperse to avoid further casualties. Meanwhile, as the southern gap had been abandoned, 3rd Royal
Tanks had started to move on to the centre also. They
too were ordered to disperse.

While this was going on, the Staffordshire Yeomanry
passed through the northern gap and continued to advance
slowly, dealing with several enemy posts and anti-tank guns
on the way. However the confusion caused by the bombing,
the blazing lorries and the constant shelling on the centre
route persuaded Custance at one o'clock to recommend to
Gatehouse that his brigade's advance should be abandoned.

Gatehouse passed this on to Lumsden with a strong recom-
mendation that it should be accepted. At half past two Lumsden told de Guingand that he was inclined to agree. The
latter decided that, in spite of Montgomery's dislike of
being disturbed, this was a critical moment at which he
must intervene. He summoned Lumsden and Leese to
confer with Montgomery at half past three, and then woke
his master up and told him what was happening. At the
same time Custance, having received no further orders,
decided to reassemble the two regiments and send them

forward through the northern gap with 3rd Royal Tanks in front. It was an hour before they began to pass through and much later before the Sherwood Rangers started. At this time the conference in Montgomery's map-lorry had begun. Both corps commanders reported the situation as they knew it, but Lumsden was clearly unhappy as much at what the situation might be beyond the ridge as at the difficulties of crossing it. It was already known that the Staffordshire Yeomanry were through, although to the north Kenchington was still delayed by his minefield-gapping problems and Currie's tanks were meeting heavy fire and progressing only very slowly to the south. Gatehouse was suggesting that the whole operation should be abandoned and that those tanks which had already crossed the ridge should be withdrawn to it. Montgomery quietly made it perfectly clear that there was no question of this and that the original plan must be carried out, an order which he passed himself to Gatehouse on the telephone. When the meeting broke up Montgomery kept Lumsden behind, warning him that, if he and his divisional commanders were not determined to break out, others would be found who were.

Soon after five o'clock Kenchington, ignorant of the high-level drama that had recently been enacted, was at last able to move his tanks through the minefield in front of them. 47th Royal Tanks went first, followed by 41st, who came up on their right to their objective just as it was getting light at a quarter past six, the 45th remaining in reserve on the ridge behind.

On the extreme left Currie's tanks had got two miles beyond the ridge and were a mile south of 26th New Zealand battalion, instead of three miles to the south-west as they should have been. Between them and the Staffordshire Yeomanry there was a gap of two and a half miles, which 3rd Royal Tanks began to fill soon after five o'clock. Behind them the Sherwood Rangers were passing through the minefield when Custance received orders from Gatehouse, passing on orders given by Lumsden after his conference with Montgomery. These were that, while Kenchington was to advance and be on his objective at dawn, Custance was to send one regiment only forward to help Currie, while the other two stayed on the ridge, where they were to be joined by Lee's infantry. This order was given before it was known that the two regiments had started to move forward to join the Staffordshire Yeomanry. At about the time it was received, the latter had come up against heavy anti-tank fire, lost six tanks and could find no hull-down position from which to fire. As it was getting light, Custance ordered all three regiments to withdraw behind the ridge, which they managed to do by seven o'clock.

Gatehouse had left at six to go up to the ridge, telling his headquarters to move an hour later to beyond the old forward British minefield. He did not realise the true situation of 8th Armoured Brigade until he got up there. At this time also there was some considerable doubt as to the real position of Kenchington's two forward regiments. They reported themselves to be on 'Pierson' two miles west of the ridge, but doubt was cast on this, and, in order to clear it up, the brigade major set off with two tanks to verify it. He found that in fact they had only got 1,000 yards beyond the ridge, and, when he himself tried to go further, both tanks were hit, one set on fire and both the officers wounded. The two regiments stayed where they were, engaging what targets they could see and being heavily shelled; 150 prisoners were picked up behind them.

By this time Currie was having a similar experience. The divisional cavalry had withdrawn behind the ridge, while 3rd Hussars and the Warwickshire Yeomanry were in a shallow valley without cover in full view of enemy tanks and anti-tank guns, well sited on a low ridge 1,000 yards to the west of them, which was their original objective, according to one disputed version of their orders. Currie said he would not advance until he had refuelled and done some maintenance; he suggested withdrawing behind Miteiriya Ridge to do this. Freyberg decided that they were to stay where they were 'to discourage enemy counter-attacks'. For a long time their position was in doubt. In fact their left was 1,000 yards in front of the extreme right of the South Africans.

At a quarter past seven 8th Army had sent a reminder to 10th Corps that the armour was to get through west of the minefields 'in order to be able to manœuvre, to locate and destroy the enemy's armoured battle groups, and to ensure that the operations of the New Zealand Division south-west from Miteiriya Ridge were not interfered with by enemy armour from the west'. Three hours later, still on the assumption that his orders had been complied with, Montgomery amplified them. Clearly ignorant that 8th Armoured Brigade had withdrawn to the ridge, he gave orders that the Sherwood Rangers were to move south-west, so that the brigade should form a line with 3rd Royal Tanks on the right, the Staffordshire Yeomanry in the centre and the Sherwood Rangers on the left, which he called 'The Hinge'. Lee was to relieve Kippenberger's brigade on the ridge, and the latter was to follow Currie in exploitation to the south. Gatehouse was to command 'The Hinge', handing Kenchington over to Briggs, who was then to 'act offensively against enemy armoured battle groups' with both 2nd and 24th Brigades.

Briggs himself believed up to about ten o'clock that Fisher was on 'Pierson' and in touch with Kenchington on his left. Shortly afterwards Fisher reported that in fact his brigade was about 1,000 yards short. The Bays had begun to move west as soon as it was light, but, when their leading squadron quickly lost eight Shermans from 88-mm. gun fire, the regiment had withdrawn and halted on orders from Fisher. On their left 9th Lancers had lost two tanks and conformed to the movement of the Bays. 10th Hussars were told to try and outflank the ridge from which the enemy's fire came, but their attack was postponed when it appeared that the enemy were preparing to counter-attack.

This was the situation when, after a talk with Alexander who had arrived to pay him a visit, Montgomery left his headquarters at half past eleven to meet the two Corps Commanders again at Freyberg's headquarters. There he decided to abandon his plan for the New Zealanders to 'exploit to the south', as he realised that it would cost too much. His new orders were that 30th Corps was to hold Miteiriya Ridge firmly and the New Zealanders were not to operate southwards. Instead the Australians were to start 'crumbling' to the north. 10th Corps was to operate westwards from 1st Armoured Division's bridgehead, 10th Armoured Division, less 24th Brigade, being withdrawn from the New Zealand sector for this. Apart from this change, Lumsden's task remained as it had been given at the conference at half past three that morning. All three corps were to patrol to ensure that any sign of enemy withdrawal was detected. These orders were confirmed on his return to his headquarters with some changes. The Australian attack was to start that night. The New Zealanders were to send strong patrols to investigate signs of enemy withdrawal on their front and Currie's brigade was to 'be offensive'. 10th Armoured Division was to be withdrawn for reorganisation, handing Kenchington's brigade over to Briggs, who was then to push forward to his original objectives.

While preoccupied with this crisis in the battle in the north, Montgomery had been faced with a major decision as to whether or not to continue the attempt to force 7th Armoured Division through the minefields right down in the south. Stamer's 131st Brigade, less 1/7th Queens who were in no state for further fighting after their attack the previous night, had been placed under Harding for an attack on the night of the 24th to extend the bridgehead westward to include February minefield. After clearing two lanes, Roberts was to pass through, followed by Roddick whose 4th Light Armoured Brigade would come up on his right. They would then get on with the original plan. Stamer and his commanding officers had met Harding at eleven and been taken up for a look at the front in a tank. Battalions had been warned at mid-day and arrangements made for 1/5th Queens on the right and 1/6th on the left to meet the minefield gapping parties at six o'clock, after marching in one case for three and a half and in the other for five miles. There was a muddle over this and zero hour was twice delayed, the attack eventually starting at half past ten. Both battalions reached their objectives beyond February without great difficulty, but were then pinned down by machine-gun fire at close range. The ground was hard and they could only dig with difficulty lying down. The battalions had about 170 casualties each, 1/6th losing their colonel, adjutant and two company commanders. Gaps were completed on both routes by half past two, but the intensity of fire on the northern one prevented the sappers from marking the sides with coils of dannert wire as well as lights. 4th County of London Yeomanry lost 4 Grants and 22 Crusaders in trying to pass through this gap, casualties including the colonel, second-in-command, adjutant and one squadron commander. Some of them went on mines before being hit by an 88-mm. which was firing along the western edge of February from the south. This led to reports that the gap had not been properly cleared.

1st Royal Tanks experienced the same difficulties on the southern routes, although their casualties were lighter. Harding, down in the area of the minefields himself, had abandoned his tank and taken to a jeep, driven by his ADC who was killed beside him. At a quarter past four he decided to postpone further attempts to get on until it was light, when he hoped to deal with the anti-tank guns by observed artillery fire and get the engineers to clear the gaps again.

The minefield gapping parties could not be reassembled till seven, when it would be broad daylight. Before this Lieutenant-Colonel Withers, the Commander Royal Engineers, convinced that they were already clear, said it could not be done in daylight. Harding told him to supervise it personally. Having made a formal protest, he went to the southern gap, called for volunteers and set off with them escorted by three tanks. At the entrance to the northern gap he found the fire so heavy that he ordered the rest of the party to withdraw, while he himself got into a tank and the commander of 21st Field Squadron into another. They then set off to drive through the gap. The first tank was hit five times but not penetrated, emerged on the far side, turned round and came back. When almost back again, one of the tanks had a track blown off and had to be abandoned.

Withers was now able to tell Harding that the tanks which had been blown up on mines were outside the lane, and that there could be no doubt that it was the very accurate anti-tank fire at the exits which had caused the casualties. The fire was so heavy that it was out of the question to lift mines by hand. Harding accepted this and decided to abandon further attempts to get the tanks forward. The Queens had no option but to stay motionless where they were. Roberts was told to keep his tanks between January and February to support them, except the battered County of London Yeomanry, who were allowed to move east of January.

Horrocks confirmed this decision when he met Harding and Roberts at eight o'clock. Back at his own headquarters, he tried to get on to Montgomery, but the latter was busy with Alexander. He spoke to de Guingand instead and told him that there was no sign of enemy withdrawal. Two alternatives presented themselves: to use the last remaining reserve, Whistler's 132nd Brigade, in a further attempt to break through February, or to abandon it and attack the western end of Munassib east of the minefields with Nichols' 50th Division, supported by Roddick. He preferred the latter. Even if Whistler was successful, the problem of getting the tanks forward would remain and 7th Armoured Division might lose heavily in the process. The other plan ran less risk, but might perhaps lead to finding another way through. Half and hour later de Guingand rang back to say that Montgomery also preferred the second alternative. He realised that some casualties were inevitable, but wished to emphasise that 7th Armoured Division must be kept 'in being'.

Morshead had foreseen the task given to his Australians and, as early as the morning of the 24th had told Whitehead, commanding 26th Brigade, to be prepared to capture the spur north of him which culminated in Point 29. This dominated the division's area and also overlooked the ground to the north up to the railway. It was therefore a valuable observation post to either side. Patrols that night had established that there were no mines between 2/48th battalion and the spur. At dusk an enemy reconnaissance party had been captured, which included the commander of 125th Infantry Regiment and that of its 2nd battalion which held the spur. The latter spoke freely under interrogation and confirmed the information, also supported by captured maps, which showed that 1st battalion of the regiment was between the road and the railway and 3rd battalion on the coast.

Whitehead had only two battalions, 2/48th and 2/24th, 2/23rd being in divisional reserve. However 40th Royal Tanks with 30 Valentines was to support them, as was the whole divisional artillery reinforced by two field and two medium regiments. They were to fire 14,508 rounds of 25-pounder and 1,066 rounds of 5½-inch shell, apart from counter-battery and 'on call' tasks. In spite of delay in relief by 2/17th due to shelling, 2/48th crossed the start line punctually and by twenty to ten had captured the first objective, 1,000 yards to the north, which was to be the start line for 2/24th. Meanwhile 2/48th's leading company drove straight through in carriers, covering 1,000 yards in nine minutes to arrive at Point 29 on the heels of the artillery bombardment, taking the enemy completely by surprise. After a short sharp hand-to-hand battle the position was secured by two o'clock. Attempts to exploit to the north were met with strong opposition, but they were well established before dawn.

All went well with 2/24th for the first 800 yards, but after that resistance stiffened and the leading infantry fell a long way behind the artillery programme. As a result casualties mounted and the attack came to a halt. While the leading company commanders were concerting a plan to get things going again, the commanding officer decided to call it off, as time was getting short. He withdrew slightly and established the whole battalion in the area of the intermediate objective by five o'clock. This meant that 2/48th on the spur formed a narrow salient, the line held by 2/24th and the composite force to the east of them curving in a crescent between Point 29 and Tel el Eisa. On the whole however it had been a most successful attack, which gave the Australians and the considerable force of artillery which could bear on the area valuable observations in all directions, instead of themselves being overlooked: 173 Germans and 67 Italians had been captured, while the Australian casualties had not been excessive, the total since the start of the battle having now risen to just over a thousand, about a sixth of whom had been killed.

Immediately to the south things had not gone so well. Lumsden's original plan had been for Kenchington to stay where he was west of Miteiriya Ridge, and move north at first light to join Fisher, who would be advancing south of Kidney Ridge. This was to have been captured by Bosvile's riflemen while the Australians were attacking further north. It was only later that it became known that Wimberley had already laid on attacks by 1st Gordons to capture 'Aberdeen', 5th Black Watch 'Stirling' and 7th Argylls 'Nairn'. Arguments were still rife about where battalions and their objectives were. In fact 'Aberdeen' was the eastern end of Kidney Ridge. In this state of uncertainty it was impossible to make proper use of the artillery, and in any case it was clearly out of the question for two different formations to attack the same place at the same time. Briggs' task was therefore altered to following up the infantry, lifting mines and helping Fisher to get forward. During the day he made several attempts to advance onto Kidney Ridge, after Littorio's tanks had themselves attacked. The Bays had lost 16 Shermans and only had 5 of them and 16 Crusaders left. The other two regiments each had about 18 Shermans and the same number of Crusaders.

Owing to a muddle over their rendezvous (they were to meet at Lee's headquarters and he had moved), Kenchington did not meet Briggs until a quarter to six in the evening. It was decided that it was impossible for his brigade to stay west of Miteiriya Ridge all night and move north from there: their 83 Shermans and 48 Crusaders were therefore withdrawn behind the ridge after dark, having had an uneventful day in which they had been shelled off and on most of the time. Attempts to find a northward route east of the ridge proved fruitless, and the whole brigade moved right back to Springbok road and then up Star track to join Briggs. It took them all night, their third without sleep, and they were exhausted on arrival.

At eleven o'clock 1st Gordons began their advance to 'Aberdeen', where they thought that part of their 'D' company already was. The rest of 'D' company, after various vicissitudes, eventually joined them, apparently on the right front of 7th Rifle Brigade. 'B' company on the left went too far south, got into trouble with enemy firing from derelict British tanks, could not find 'D' and came back to where they had started. Further south 5th Black Watch met hardly any opposition in attacking 'Stirling'. To the south again a much weakened 7th Argylls captured 'Nairn', their three companies reduced to a total of 100 men, two of them having no officers at all.

At twenty past four Wimberley suggested to Leese that Briggs should take advantage of this and switch his advance to the south, as 'Aberdeen' had clearly not been taken. This was passed on to 10th Corps who refused, but told both armoured brigades to 'make contact with 5th Black Watch on Stirling to see if they could help 51st Division'. At about half past seven Lumsden told Briggs to move Fisher north-west to an area in which he could protect the left flank of the Australians. This was not found possible, and the brigade remained very much where it had been the day before.

Way down south in 13th Corps 69th Brigade's attack on the western end of Munassib had been a costly failure. In several ways it resembled the attack 131st Brigade had made in the same area after Alam el Halfa, and with much the same result. This virtually brought active operations in the south to an end. Hughes, whose two brigades had now suffered a total of some 700 casualties, took over defence of the front south of Munassib with the Free French under command, and 7th Armoured Division, with 70 Grants, 27 Crusaders and 50 Stuarts, was withdrawn behind the minefields.

9 SECOND THOUGHTS

October 26th – 28th

Early on the 26th Montgomery realised that he must think again. He therefore spent all morning, and in fact most of the day, in careful consideration of what to do next. Althougi. 30th Corps had nearly reached its original final objective and only minor operations were needed to complete this task, casualties were mounting, being by now over 4,500 in addition to the 500 in 10th Corps and 1,000 in 13th. This was not excessive, but there were no reinforcements for the South Africans or for the New Zealanders, who with 800 casualties had lost a third of their fighting strength. The Highland Division's figure had now risen to 2,100 and the Corps had need of rest if it were to make another major effort.

The enemy's casualties were more difficult to assess. 2,000 prisoners had been taken, of whom just over 600 were German. The respective losses of the Germans and Italians were assessed by intelligence to be: in men, 32,000 and 29,000; in tanks, 250 and 280; in field guns, 140 and 200; in 88-mm. 50 and 40; and in other anti-tank guns, 400 and 320. These were very high figures and, if true, would have meant that there was practically nothing for 8th Army to fight against, which was not borne out by the experience of the troops in the front line.

10th Corps had undoubtedly inflicted losses on the enemy's tanks, but had not yet broken out into mine-free country. 13th Corps had shot its bolt, and the momentum of the whole attack was diminishing. 8th Army intelligence believed that there had been no significant change in the dispositions of 15th and 21st Panzer Divisions or of 90th Light, which was thought still to be near Daba. A document captured before the battle had stated that Stumme's policy was to wear down the British attacks without carrying out large-scale counter-attacks with tanks. It looked as if this policy was being followed and that the Panzer divisions would not launch their full strength, until either 10th Corps broke out or the enemy infantry had been so weakened as to be unable to resist further in the north.

They did not know that Stumme was missing nor that Rommel had arrived back the night before. Field-Marshal Keitel had rung him up at Semmering on the afternoon of the 24th with what news there was, which included the disappearance of Stumme. Rommel had remained in a state of suspense and anxiety, until Hitler rang him up after midnight and asked him to fly back. He flew to Rome early next morning, where he received a very gloomy report of the logistic situation. Only three daily issues of petrol remained in Africa instead of the thirty which he had demanded as the minimum. He was indignant, and realised that there was little hope of a successful outcome to the battle. Having flown across the Mediterranean, he reached Panzer Armee as daylight was fading, met by the faithful Westphal and by von Thoma, who had temporarily taken over command since Stumme had been missing. They painted a grim picture. Shortage of petrol was acute and had prevented any major movement. Limited counter-attacks by the armour deployed behind the threatened sectors were all that could be done. 15th Panzer Division had been continuously employed in this way, and that evening was reduced to only 31 tanks fit for action. The intense British artillery fire and the air attacks, which had never ceased night and day, had caused terrible losses and were seriously affecting morale.

Rommel decided that his aim for the next few days must be to throw the British out of his main defence line at all costs, and to eliminate the dangerous salient which was being created in the area of Kidney Ridge. It was on this area that his attention was focused, and the Australian attack on Point 29 that night seems to have caused him much less concern than the Highland Division's attacks and the subsequent cautious attempt by 2nd Armoured Brigade to exploit them. He was up at five in the morning of the 26th and went off to watch the counter-attacks which 15th Panzer and Littorio were to make on Kidney Ridge. He was disappointed in the slowness of the attack and impressed with the fierceness of the British resistance, the intensity of the artillery fire and the ceaseless air attacks by fighters and light bombers, which had caused him so much trouble at Alam el Halfa.

Realising that little progress was being made and sensing that 8th Army was 'continually feeding fresh forces into the attack on Hill 28', he decided to move up von Sponeck's 90th Light Division and the *Kampfstaffel*, the battle group which protected his own headquarters, to reinforce the attack. To von Thoma's Afrika Korps it seemed that the British were making repeated attempts to break out with tanks south of Hill 28, that is in the area of Kidney Ridge. The climax came in the afternoon when a thrust by 160 tanks wiped out a battalion of 164th Division and penetrated southwards. This led to violent fighting, in which 15th Panzer Division and Littorio, with their few remaining tanks, forced the British back. By the end of the day the toll of tanks totally destroyed in the two divisions in the three days of battle had mounted to 61 and 56 respectively.

This picture of a day's furious fighting bears little if any relation to that seen by his opponents. After his attempts to move north-west early in the day, Briggs made no further effort to advance and reported the day as one of heavy shelling with no movement. It is true that Kenchington did move up to the left of Fisher in the afternoon, but it was in no way an attempt to advance against opposition. Similarly the Australians to the north reported constant threats of counter-attack against Point 29 all day, involving as many as 100 tanks; but they were dispersed by artillery fire and air attacks. The move of 46th Royal Tanks, the reserve regiment of 23rd Armoured Brigade, to join the 40th in this sector was no doubt one of the 'repeated attempts by enemy tanks' or the 'continual feeding in of fresh forces'.

While Rommel was flinging all his reserves in the north into a desperate attempt to restore the situation, Montgomery was calmly thinking things over in his map-lorry under the impression that it was a quiet day. At about mid-day he issued new orders. Wimberley was to clear up any enemy still resisting up to the limit of the original objectives. Morshead was to carry out a further attack in the north on the night of the 28th, that is after a pause of three days from his attack of the previous night. Apart from these, Leese's operations were to be limited to minor ones to help Lumsden to break out. He was to make his sector secure against enemy attack of any kind and be prepared to undertake major operations later.

Lumsden was to have responsibility for the security of Leese's bridgehead, but was to 'make progress' west and north-west of Kidney Ridge, while the RAF continued to attack the enemy armour. Horrocks was to make certain that 7th Armoured Division did not suffer any further casualties from offensive action. That evening Montgomery held a conference to decide on the regrouping to provide a reserve for Leese's next major operation. His main aim was to get the New Zealand Division free, and a warning was also given that Harding was to be prepared to move north.

Lumsden had received Montgomery's new orders by three o'clock, and gave new ones of his own accordingly. Bosvile was to attack at eleven o'clock that night in the area of Kidney Ridge, supported by all the artillery of 10th Corps and some of 30th's. 2nd/60th were to capture 'Woodcock' which included Point 33, 2,000 yards north-west of 7th Rifle Brigade and 1,000 west of 2/13th Australian battalion. On the left 2nd Rifle Brigade, relieved from the minefield task force that afternoon, were to capture 'Snipe', a low ridge 2,000 yards west of Kidney Ridge. The brigade was to lift mines for itself and form an anti-tank screen at dawn, through which Fisher, followed by Kenchington, was to advance at half past four to the north-west, the two brigades together now restored to a strength of 120 Grants or Shermans and 80 Crusaders.

Lack of time and the usual arguments about where people and their objectives were greatly hindered the preparation of the artillery fire programme. 1st Armoured had at last recognised that the Highland Division had been right all the time, a bitter pill for desert veterans to swallow; but this did not eliminate differences of opinion at lower levels. The 60th had a very difficult approach march on Moon track, as the moon was not yet up and the dust was appalling. As a result they went too far south and did not get as far west as they thought they had. The leading company reported that it had reached 'Woodcock', but the rest were held up and tried to move round to the right, capturing some anti-tank guns on the way. At first light the colonel decided that their position was untenable, and withdrew north-eastwards until they were 1,000 yards north of Kidney Ridge and the same distance short of their objective.

Lieutenant-Colonel Vic Turner, commanding the 2nd Rifle Brigade, had been warned in the morning of his probable task and had tried to have a look at the area of attack; but dust, smoke, enemy shelling and considerable doubt about both the true position of the observation post and the intentions of the local Highlanders made the reconnaissance of little value. However a narrow start line was found before it was dark. Doubt as to its position led the colonel to give an alternative order for the direction to be taken in case the opening barrage came down somewhere else, a sensible precaution which in the event proved necessary. 'A' company was late on the start line and 'C' had to start alone on the left, motor platoons on foot following a screen of carriers in front. The sixteen 6-pounders of 'S' company and the eleven of 239 Battery 76th Anti-tank Regiment Royal Artillery were to drive forward from the start line when the objectives had been taken, which they were at a quarter past midnight, little opposition having been met. Unfortunately, when they started, the medical officer and his ambulance were away treating casualties from bombing. They got left behind and were unable to rejoin. There were long ridges of soft sand to negotiate and many vehicles never made the journey, but finally thirteen of the Rifle Brigade's own 6-pounders and six of the gunners' got there, with ammunition for the machine-guns and rations and water for the position. The vehicles set off back again with Pearson, the second-in-command, just before it was light. Before then the observation post officer of 2nd RHA had disappeared, leaving his vehicle behind. He eventually turned up with 7th Rifle Brigade, and his absence was to be sorely felt throughout the day.

An excursion by 'C' Company's carriers to the ridge south-west of the position stirred up a hornet's nest, having penetrated into a leaguer of Italian tanks and trucks. There was also a German leaguer clearly visible 1,000 yards to the north. They both started to move west at daylight and offered excellent targets, a total of 14 'knock-outs' being claimed. The battalion was disposed in an oval, the ends of which were north-east and south-west of battalion headquarters in a German dug-out in the centre, and was divided into three segments. 'A' company with ten 6-pounders held the north-east, 'C' with four the western and 'B' with six the south-east.

Uncertainty about the fate of the 60th had caused delay in the move forward of the armour. Kenchington's brigade, who were still very tired having not had a decent night's sleep since the battle started, were told to begin their advance through the Rifle Brigade at ten to six. There was a long delay in collecting their leading regiment, 47th Royal Tanks, and it did not get going until nearly half past seven. Their first action was to start firing at the Rifle Brigade, probably aiming at derelict tanks lying near them. The rest of the Brigade joined in, until Lieutenant Wintour drove over in a carrier to stop them. They then advanced, while the Rifle Brigade opened fire on 25 German tanks forming up on the ridge to the south-west. When the 47th reached 'Snipe' at half past eight, they were fiercely engaged and 6 of their tanks were soon ablaze. A good deal of smoke was used, but it seems to have been as much a hindrance as a help. After repeated attempts to make headway, the 47th with only 5 Shermans and 6 Crusaders left were withdrawn behind the ridge, a mile east of the Rifle Brigade. The 41st had had no success in getting forward further to the left and lost 12 tanks: the 45th had not moved. Meanwhile the Rifle Brigade felt keenly the lack of means of getting artillery support, particularly when attacked first by 13 Italian tanks from the west and then by a group of about 25 German tanks, which were crossing the southern flank to attack Kenchington's. Eight of this group were claimed. The anti-tank gun position at 'Snipe' was now serious, with only four guns left in each sector and ammunition very short for those facing west and south-west.

At about one o'clock another group of nine Italian tanks attacked again in the south, after the whole position had been heavily shelled, causing a considerable number of casualties. The only gun which could be brought to bear was Sergeant Calistan's. He manned it, while Turner loaded and observed and the platoon commander, Lieutenant Toms, acted as 'Number One'. The colonel told Calistan to hold his fire until the tanks were 600 yards away. Six were hit and set on fire, but there were now only two or three rounds left. Toms ran to his jeep 100 yards away and drove back with ammunition, all in a hail of machine-gun fire from the remaining three tanks which continued to advance, setting the jeep on fire 10 yards from the gun. Turner and Toms unloaded it, carried the ammunition to the gun and reloaded, Turner being wounded in the head. He was persuaded against his will to lie down, while Calistan took careful aim and knocked out all three. Toms was wounded soon afterwards.

Although the north flank had not been attacked so heavily, it could not be neglected, as neither the position of the 60th nor that of Fisher's brigade gave it much protection. For a long time nobody knew for certain where the 60th were, and it was not finally cleared up until the Bays made contact with them late in the morning. Fisher had made slow progress since he started at six. At first, when 9th Lancers picked up about 60 German prisoners, it was thought that the enemy had withdrawn, but they soon found themselves up against the usual opposition. Reports by 10th Hussars of heavy movement northwards on the Rahman track and rumours of the arrival of von Randow's 21st Panzer Division all imposed caution. By mid-day it was clear that the Germans still held Point 33 in 'Woodcock'. The Bays were a mile east of them, and the brigade's position stretched southwest from there to just north of the east end of Kidney Ridge, the 60th being between the Bays and 9th Lancers. They claimed to have destroyed 12 German and 2 Italian tanks and four 88-mm. guns by this time. At half past one the Bays were told to capture Point 33 and were given the troop of three Churchills to help them. The attack began an hour later. One of the Churchills was quickly knocked out by an 88-mm. and the other two retired, their guns being out of action. The attack was called off, and a defensive posture assumed when information was received of an impending enemy attack. This never materialised, although some tanks attacked 10th Hussars shortly before, being driven off with the loss of three.

There was then a lull in the battle until four o'clock when the main enemy attack started. The night before Rommel had decided to move 21st Panzer Division and half the army artillery up from the south, well knowing that he would not have the petrol to send them back again. They were to join 15th Panzer, Littorio and part of Ariete in an attack in the Kidney Ridge area, while 90th Light, supported by all the Stukas available, was to attack the Australians. 90th Light and Trieste had been moved up to the south of Sidi Abd el Rahman during the night, but continuous bombing attacks had delayed the move north of 21st Panzer and Ariete. Forming up, watched by Rommel himself, was interfered with by further bombing and artillery fire. At four o'clock (8th Army time) the attack was launched. It was met by 'murderous fire', losses were heavy and they were forced to withdraw. That evening both the Panzer divisions and 90th Light had to find more troops to help hold the defensive screen. This setback made Rommel almost lose hope, and in the letter he wrote to his wife that night he spoke of the probability of defeat and the possibility that he himself would not survive it.

To Fisher's tanks this grand attack appeared to be no more than an attempt by two groups of about 40 tanks each to advance south of 'Woodcock' and then again an hour later against 10th Hussars, presenting their right flank to the Rifle Brigade, apparently oblivious of the latter's presence. They were stopped and withdrew, after 10th Hussars had claimed 12 and the Rifle Brigade 13, most of them falling to the guns of the anti-tank battery. By half past five the attack was over, but the southern group continued to attack and pour fire into the Rifle Brigade's position until long after dark.

By this time a message, confused because the codes had

been destroyed, had been received from Bosvile to say that the battalion would be relieved 'at the fashionable time for dinner'. After dark the adjutant, being the senior unwounded officer, decided to evacuate all the wounded. The remainder would stay to hand over, but if attacked were given discretion to withdraw by companies. No relief came and the transport did not reappear. At half past ten 'A' and 'B' companies started to withdraw, just as concentrations of our own artillery started landing on the enemy leaguer 1,200 yards to the north-west. The tanks and other vehicles thus disturbed moved straight for 'Snipe', and at a quarter past eleven battalion headquarters and the remainder left, arriving without incident in the main position.

The Rifle Brigade claimed to have knocked out 76 tanks or self-propelled guns: 27 were found when the area was examined after the whole battle had passed on and expert assessment put the final figure at 37. Even the reduced figure was a remarkable feat, to which Turner's Victoria Cross and Calistan's Distinguished Conduct Medal and many other decorations were a fitting tribute. Rommel himself described it as 'a tremendously powerful anti-tank defence'.

The artillery fire which had driven the German tanks towards 'Snipe' in the middle of the night had been in support of renewed attempts by 1st Armoured Division to capture 'Woodcock' and 'Snipe', this time with Lee's lorried infantry. Briggs at first thought that the Rifle Brigade had been overrun, but later believed them to have withdrawn, having run out of ammunition. As late as half past four there was 'still no news of them', and the true situation was not known until eight in the morning.

Meanwhile a hastily prepared attack had been laid on with all three of Lee's battalions. 4th Royal Sussex had a bad start when they got into a fight with 1st Gordons at 'Aberdeen'. One company was then almost destroyed when it went to attack what was probably a German tank leaguer. After an advance of two miles, in which 200 prisoners and five 88-mm. guns had been captured, the colonel decided that he was on his objective. It was then half past one: the ground was very hard and digging difficult. He was completely out of touch with brigade and everybody else. Shortly after dawn, still not properly dug in and in a very exposed position north-west of Kidney Ridge, they were attacked by German tanks, which methodically knocked out all the anti-tank guns first. At half past seven they closed in and half an hour later the 300 survivors were marched off, casualties having been about 60.

While this had been going on the Yorkshire Dragoons to the north had had a squadron overrun and been forced to withdraw. To the south 2nd Royal Sussex were on Kidney Ridge pinned down by heavy fire, but otherwise all right, although their colonel was killed. The 5th battalion was in much the same plight, but had not got as far west as the Rifle Brigade had been the day before. Lieutenant John Montgomery, intelligence officer of the 2nd Royal Sussex, wrote in his diary:

Quite early in the morning the colonel went off in his carrier to visit the forward companies, a distance of about 300 yards in front. It would have been wiser of him to have walked, for the presence of his carrier carrying a flag undoubtedly attracted the attention of the enemy. As I was on the telephone at the time I noted where he had gone and a few minutes later set off in the direction of 'A' company, which held the forward right flank positions.

The route to 'A' company involved the crossing of a minefield, in which there was always a possible anti-personnel mine. From here I walked across to a slit trench full of anti-tank gunners, and from there the route struck off to the right to 'A' company on the far side of the ridge. There was considerable cover here, small scrub bushes and some dead ground making it impossible to see over the ridge. The journey was slow, mainly because I had both to look around and also keep an eye on the ground in case of trip-wires or anti-personnel mines. I was within 100 yards of 'A' company when two bullets whizzed past my head. There was no doubt that they were meant for me; I dropped to the ground at once and began to carry out the old battle drill of 'crawl – observe', just as we had done hundreds of times during exercises in Kent. Only this time it seemed a little more realistic.

From the ground I could see nothing, and was convinced I was out of sight of the marksman. But I was not convinced that this was the best route to 'A' company. I therefore started to crawl back and a few minutes later dropped into the trench amongst our anti-tank gunners. Roy Leywood, heavily moustached and unshaven, greeted me. 'You know the colonel's dead?' he asked. This news rather staggered me, and for a moment I felt lost. I had been with the colonel all the time, and now that he had gone there seemed a great change in the battle. I could not for some time afterwards realise that Kenneth Hooper, whom we had all known so well, as company commander, second-in-command, and then as an extremely young and energetic battalion commander was dead.

The circumstances of his death I heard later from Keith Tucker, who as a company commander was at his headquarters when Kenneth Hooper came up in his carrier. The colonel got out of the carrier, jumped down into the slit trench and began to talk to Keith Tucker. At this point Tucker warned him that it wasn't safe to stand up because the top of the trench was in full view of some snipers in front. There was also what looked like an anti-tank gun some way over to the right. The colonel now said he would like to have a look, and although Keith Tucker again warned him it was risky, he insisted on standing up and leaning over the front of the trench. From there he could see some of the enemy positions and was able to get his bearings. At this moment Tucker, who was also looking over the top of the trench, turned and saw the colonel fall heavily to the ground. He jumped down to pick him up and found he had been shot through the forehead, and was dead.

Little of all this situation was accurately known at higher levels, even by Lee himself, although a number of reports from Fisher's tanks told of prisoners being marched off to the west from where 4th Royal Sussex were thought to be. At first light 9th Lancers had advanced to Point 33, the Bays also turning up there later. But at ten to seven the brigade was told to stand fast, as plans at higher levels were being changed and Gatehouse was to take over the front. They withdrew slightly and had breakfast, just about the time when both 4th Royal Sussex and the Yorkshire Dragoons were being overrun. This naturally led to considerable bitterness and recrimination.

In fact Montgomery had for the moment decided to abandon the attempt to break through in the Kidney Ridge area. He held a conference with Leese, Lumsden and their Chiefs of Staff at eight o'clock that morning, October 28th, at which he decided that 'Woodcock – Snipe' was to become a defensive front, held temporarily by Gatehouse and then by Leese. 1st Armoured Division was to be withdrawn as soon as possible to rest and reorganise. Lumsden had to be prepared to exploit westwards from the flank of the Australian attack to be launched that night. It was now clear that 21st Panzer Division had moved north, and the RAF were to continue to attack targets in the area of Tel el Aqqaqir, where the Afrika Korps was now thought to be concentrated. Later in the day orders were given for Harding, leaving Roddick behind, to move up to near El Alamein station.

Freyberg, who two days before had been proposing 'a new attack on a three-divisional front, using the armour to provide a "firm base" by protecting the flanks and only joining battle if the enemy armour attacked away from his gun line', went to see Morshead that morning and then went on to lunch with Montgomery. The latter told him that he planned to use the New Zealand Division to advance along the coast in exploitation of the Australian attack, Freyberg to use his armoured brigade to protect his left flank. 6th New Zealand Brigade would take over the Australian sector the night following the one of the latter's attack, that is the 29th-30th. Freyberg's attack would begin as soon as possible afterwards, probably the next night, the 30th-31st. As the New Zealanders themselves could not provide any more infantry, he would be fed with a succession of British infantry brigades, first the 151st of 50th Division, then 152nd of the Highland, then 131st of the 44th and finally perhaps the Greek brigade. Currie's 9th Armoured Brigade would have first priority for replacement tanks.

While Montgomery was thus changing the point of his main

thrust, Rommel was under the erroneous impression that attacks were made in the northern sector in the morning, thrown back to their starting point each time by the Panzers, who again lost heavily in tanks, and that in the afternoon a concentration for the final decisive break-through was in progress. Almost all remaining German units were moved up from the south, the whole of the Afrika Korps was committed to holding the line and Rommel told all commanders that the decisive moment had come; it was a battle of life or death, and each man must give of his best.

The true point of the thrust became clear soon after ten o'clock that night when the Australian attack began. Its plan was ambitious, involving all three brigades, supported by 224 field and 48 medium guns. In the first phase Windeyer's 20th Brigade, holding Point 29 with 2/17th battalion, were to advance two miles north with 2/15th and then extend the area captured 2,000 yards to the east with 2/13th, 40th Royal Tanks facing west between 2/17th and 2/15th to repel counter-attacks. In the next phase, Whitehead's 26th Brigade was to capture the area between the present most northerly positions and the salt-marsh immediately east of the road which ran along the ridge, itself just east of the railway. This meant capturing a considerable area, including the strong-point of Thompson's Post. Finally Godfrey's 24th Brigade, already east of the railway, was to extend its position north-westwards to join up with 26th Brigade.

Windeyer's attack went well in spite of difficulties caused by an unexpected and heavily booby-trapped minefield on 2/13th's front and by shelling of 2/15th's forming-up area, in which both the commanding officer and the adjutant were wounded. Very soon after midnight they were on their objectives, digging in and laying mines to protect themselves.

In 26th Brigade 2/23rd were to capture the area of the main road about two miles north-east of 2/15th's objective. 2/24th were to capture Thompson's Post immediately north-east of 2/13th. As no mines were expected, 2/23rd were to repeat the method which had worked so well in the previous attack and drive straight to the objective in carriers and on the tanks of 46th Royal Tanks. Unfortunately the route to the

start line was a very complicated one, involving three changes
of direction, and the attack beyond it meant a final eastward
turn when they reached the railway. There was no moon,
a great deal of dust and a certain amount of artillery and
machine-gun fire before they reached the start line, by
which time three tanks had already been lost on mines.

The attack started at twenty to midnight and was immediately held up, as they could not find the gaps in 2/17th's
own protective minefield. These were eventually cleared and,
after an advance of 600 yards, they came under heavy fire
from anti-tank and machine guns and also ran on to scattered
mines. The infantry jumped off the tanks and the two lost
touch with each other. The colonel of 2/23rd led forward
as many men as he could find, which was only about 70,
and some claim to have reached the railway before they
were forced back. The tank commanding officer tried to
regain control, all the squadrons having diverged and run
into trouble. He eventually found that he had only twelve
tanks left, including the four of his own headquarters. He
had just ordered one squadron to send three forward, when
he and two other officers were wounded by mortar fire and
orders were received from the infantry colonel to withdraw
and organise positions to meet counter-attack, the latter
having decided that it was too late to get the attack going
again. There was now little time left before daylight and
at ten to five Morshead decided to call the whole attack
off. Casualties on the whole had not been heavy and most
of the large number of tanks lost were recovered.

Rommel described the weight of the attack as 'something
quite exceptional' and gave credit to his artillery for bringing
it to a halt after the battle 'had raged with tremendous fury
for six hours'. He had himself spent the night on the coast
road, while he moved his headquarters further to the rear.
He paced up and down, turning over in his mind whether or
not to take the fateful decision to retreat. He realised that it
would only invite disaster to wait until the final break-
through came; but it would inevitably mean abandoning
most of his immobile infantry. He therefore decided to make
one more attempt 'by the tenacity and stubbornness of his
defence to persuade the enemy to call off his attack'. The

chance was slim, but the petrol situation dictated the choice. If retreat was forced on him, his aim would be to get away as many tanks and weapons as he could. By dawn he had decided that, if pressure became too great, he would withdraw to Fuka, 50 miles further back, before the battle reached its climax.

October 29th – November 2nd

While Rommel was seriously contemplating the possibility of
retreat, doubts were growing at many different levels on the
other side. The battle had now lasted for six nights and five
days and did not yet seem to have achieved anything but a
mounting toll of casualties. Back in London Churchill,
undoubtedly aware of rumours circulating in Cairo, was
fretting. News of the withdrawal of the New Zealand Division
from the front line and rumours that others were being pulled
out also stirred memories of previous failures, as well as of
the First World War. Overnight the Prime Minister had
drafted a stern telegram to Alexander expressing his concern,
which was presented to Brooke while still in bed on the 29th,
and which led to a hot-tempered flare-up between them.
Churchill appeared now to regret the choice of Montgomery
and accused him of fighting only a half-hearted battle. At a
meeting of the War Cabinet and the Chiefs of Staff, held
that day to discuss the matter, Brooke had to defend Alexander and Montgomery against taunts of having done nothing
for three days and of losing their grip on the battle. He
expressed his complete confidence in the progress and handling of the battle, although privately he was not without
doubts.

It was these anxieties which brought Alexander with
Casey and McCreery to see Montgomery on the morning of
the 29th. The failure of 26th Brigade's part in the Australian
attack did not augur well for the future development of
'Supercharge', as the new plan for pushing the New Zealand
Division along the coast was called. Nevertheless Montgomery
had decided to continue with it, in spite of the doubts of
several of his own staff, including de Guingand, who felt that
it would be driving against the enemy at his strongest point.
Alexander and McCreery too seemed to share these doubts,
but could not deflect the Army Commander from his plan,

although continuation of the Australian attack was postponed until the 30th. Later in the morning, information came in which proved that all three regiments of 90th Light Division had been engaged against the Australians the night before. There was also evidence that Trieste, Rommel's last reserve, had been put into the line to the south of them. It was therefore clear that the original plan for 'Supercharge' would meet very strong opposition and had been anticipated by Rommel, who it was now known had returned. When de Guingand brought this news to Montgomery, he quickly agreed to change his plan. The Australians would still carry out their northward attack on the night of the 30th; but Freyberg, instead of passing through them, would strike west the following night, following a concentrated air attack, on a front of 4,000 yards south of Point 29 and north of Kidney Ridge, his centre line being the original northern boundary of the Highland Division. This would bring him to just east of the Rahman track, north of Tel el Aqqaqir. He was to be supported by all available artillery and reinforced with 151st and 152nd Infantry Brigades and 23rd Armoured Brigade. The whole operation would be under command of Leese. When he had reached his objectives, Freyberg was to establish a screen behind which 10th Corps could form up ready to attack the enemy. The leading tanks were to be on the line of the existing forward positions by five in the morning and were to fight their own way out, if the New Zealanders had not reached their objectives. 10th Corps was to establish itself before daylight round Tel el Aqqaqir, where it was hoped that the decisive tank battle would be fought to destroy the remains of Rommel's armour. Lumsden was then to move north-west towards Ghazal station to cut off Rommel's forces in the coastal sector. At least two armoured car regiments were to be got out at an early stage to operate on their own for two or three days behind the lines. Montgomery finished his orders with a demand for determined leadership, faith in the success of the plan, and no 'belly-aching'.

While 'Supercharge' was being rehashed, 90th Light Division was trying to reopen the way to the second battalion of its 125th Panzer Grenadier Regiment, cut off by 20th Brigade's attack. Three attempts were made during the day, all of which were beaten off without difficulty by artillery fire, of which a great deal could be brought to bear round the salient, sticking up like a thumb, in which 20th Brigade now were. Rommel did not however make any major effort to restore the situation. He was expecting Montgomery to continue with a major attack and was preoccupied with other things. Much of his attention was directed towards planning the withdrawal to the position at Fuka. It was while he was discussing this with Westphal that a report arrived from Comando Supremo saying that two British divisions had crossed the Qattara Depression and were then 60 miles south of Mersa Matruh. It was not until the following morning that the report proved to be baseless. It did not improve relations with the Italians which were already under a severe strain as the result of failure to supply petrol. On the 26th the tanker *Proserpina* of 4,809 tons had been set on fire by aerial torpedoes, the eighth ship to be disabled that month. Now came the news that on the 28th the tanker *Louisano* of 2,550 tons had also been sunk. Rommel vented his wrath at the failure of the Italian Navy to protect them on the head of the unfortunate General Barbassetti, who came to see him in place of Cavallero.

In 30th Corps feverish activity reigned in preparing for 'Supercharge', and the night of the 29th was the first for a long time in which no real attack was made. Montgomery held another conference to solve the problem of finding room for the assembly of the New Zealanders behind the front, and also for the redeployment of artillery to support the two attacks in different directions on successive nights. One minor but tiresome matter dealt with was the change of time. GHQ had ordered that the whole theatre should revert from Egypt Summer to Egypt Standard Time at midnight on the 31st, clocks being put back one hour. This would be the night of the New Zealand attack and great confusion was foreseen. Montgomery ordered that there should be no change of time within 8th Army's area until the battle was over. This avoided confusion at the front, but caused it elsewhere. The RAF were almost all based outside the area and the railway was affected too. In the end all signals from 8th Army's area had to give the time in Greenwich Mean

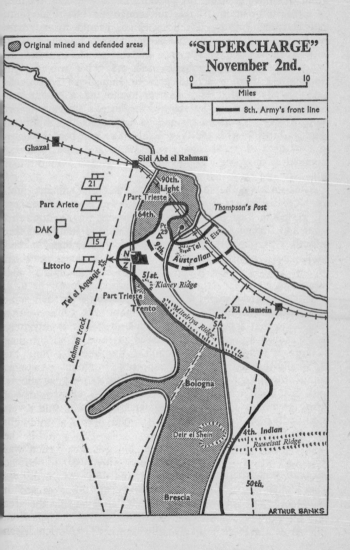

Time as well, in order to prevent, or at least to reduce, the confusion caused. At this conference it was also decided that Harding, leaving Roddick behind, should move north on the night of the 31st; that Kenchington's brigade should be withdrawn for re-equipment; that Lee should stay behind under command of Wimberley and that what was left of Gatehouse's division should pass to Lumsden's command. 24th Brigade handed its tanks over to the 2nd, a bitter blow to this brigade in its first battle, the latter's strength being brought up to 82 Shermans and 72 Crusaders. By this time Currie's brigade with the New Zealanders had been brought to a strength of 72 Shermans and Grants and 49 Crusaders. Rommel at this time had 116 German and 220 Italian tanks left.

After dark on the following night, that of October 30th, the New Zealanders began to move forward from where they had rested to their assembly area. Freyberg was up near the front and during the night was struck by the fatigue of the infantry, particularly 152nd Brigade. 151st Brigade too would have little opportunity for reconnaissance, and he became acutely aware of the difficulties of collecting all the supporting units for brigades of so many divisions. His own divisional artillery would all have to redeploy after their support of the Australians that very night. He came to the conclusion that a postponement of his attack for twenty-four hours should be seriously considered in spite of all the disadvantages including the reduction in the time of moonlight. He finally decided that it was impossible to mount his attack within forty-eight hours and asked Leese to postpone it until the night of November 1st. This was referred to 8th Army at twenty-five past eleven, and no answer was given until half past six next morning, when Montgomery most reluctantly agreed.

While this decision hung in the balance, the Australians were carrying out their attack, which amounted to nothing very different from the completion of the attack which White-head's 26th Brigade was to have carried out two nights before. The first phase was to start at ten with an attack by 2/32nd battalion north-east for two miles to the coast road from 2/15th's position in the salient. At one o'clock 2/24th on the right, mostly south of the railway, and 2/48th on the left, north of it, were to attack south-eastwards along the line of the railway and the road. In two later phases, which were to start when the second was complete, 2/48th was to clear the area north of the road to the north-east, and 2/3rd Pioneer Battalion was to clear the area between the 2/32nd and the coast.

2/32nd met stiff opposition beyond their first objectives and had great difficulty in bulldozing a gap in the railway line for their vehicles. The colonel and the second-in-command were both wounded and companies kept very close together. They were tightly packed in a small area when they finally reorganised their position astride the coast road.

This congestion delayed the 2/48th, who also had trouble with enemy posts which were still active near their start line astride the coast road. These had still not been cleared up when the artillery programme had been going for a quarter of an hour. Rather than postpone it, their colonel decided to start off as best he could. They pressed on most gallantly in spite of mounting casualties; but by quarter past four the colonel decided it was hopeless and pulled them back to the first objective. There were now so few left, only 2 officers and 72 men, that he could not even hold that, and therefore went right back to 2/32nd's position.

2/24th had also been delayed. When they could find no trace of 2/48th on the start line, they assumed that the latter had already started and so set off themselves. All went well until they were 200 yards short of their first objective, when stiff opposition was met. Their experience followed almost exactly that of 2/48th, and they also finally withdrew to join 2/32nd with only one officer and 84 men left.

2/3rd Pioneer Battalion, after a number of delays and difficulties, had crossed their start line in 2/32nd's position at twenty-five past four, but had soon been held up by artillery fire. After that, companies lost touch with each other and for a long time nobody knew what their situation was. At dawn therefore 26th Brigade, or what was left of it, was grouped in a small area about a mile from north to south and half that from east to west, astride the road and railway two miles north-east of the nearest troops of 20th Brigade and about three miles north of the rest of the division. 2/32nd battalion was the main force, the weakened remnants of 2/48th and 2/24th facing south-east and south respectively and the situation of the Pioneers to the north being extremely obscure.

The attack had surprised the enemy who were in the process of getting 21st Panzer Division free from the area by relieving it with Trieste. After one attack at seven in the morning of October 31st had been beaten off by artillery fire, 40th Royal Tanks, less 'A' Squadron which stayed with 20th Brigade, began to make their way across to join White-head. This alarmed Rommel, who immediately drove up the road and set up his command post east of the mosque at Sidi Abd el Rahman, summoning von Thoma and the latter's Chief of Staff, Bayerlein, just returned from Europe, to meet him there. Meanwhile 40th Royal Tanks, losing a number of Valentines on mines, including the commanding officer's, and under constant heavy fire, had got two troops north of the railway after much difficulty in finding a crossing. Von Thoma, who had met Rommel at eleven (8th Army time) was told to attack an hour later with 21st Panzer and 90th Light Divisions, supported by Stuka attacks and a barrage from all the artillery in the sector. When the tanks of 21st Panzer could be seen forming up to move down the railway about mid-day, the two tank squadrons of the 40th themselves crossed the railway and moved north-west towards them, supported by the 6-pounders of 289 anti-tank battery Royal Artillery. However bombing by the RAF and concentrations of artillery fire sufficed to break up the attack, which was renewed twice more at intervals of two hours. On the first occasion 18 tanks came down the railway and actually penetrated the position before being driven out by the combined efforts of the tanks, anti-tank guns and artillery, leaving five tanks and one 88-mm. behind. At four o'clock another 18 had managed to worm their way into hull-down positions on the eastern flank, from which they could engage 40th Royal Tanks from the right rear. Their colonel was away at the time meeting his brigade commander: on the way back his own and the rear link tank were knocked out by anti-tank fire from Thompson's Post. It was not realised until later that, although 'A' Squadron were moved over from 20th Brigade to help, the whole regiment had been forced to withdraw to 2/13th battalion's position two miles south of the railway. Their casualties were 9 officers and 35 men, a high proportion of the tank crews engaged.

Leese's attention had been devoted more to preparations for the New Zealand attack than to the battle round 26th Brigade. 'Strong measures' by the staffs of both 10th and 30th Corps were needed to move headquarters and units, mostly of 10th Armoured Division, to clear the areas required. That evening 8th Army considered that there were few signs of enemy withdrawal, although there was a noticeable thinning-out of vehicles in the northern sector, to which movement, as reported by the air, was confined. The Afrika Korps was thought to have its main strength north of Tel el Aqqaqir, with 90th Light Division about Sidi Abd el Rahman. 21st Panzer Division had been identified as participating in the attack on 26th Brigade, and the omens therefore appeared favourable for the main phase of 'Supercharge'. At the same time at the headquarters of the Afrika Corps von Thoma and Bayerlein had come to the conclusion that it would be better to withdraw the troops of 125th Panzer Grenadier Regiment, who were still round Thompson's Post behind 20th and 26th Brigades, accepting the loss of the heavy weapons, rather than suffer heavy losses and commit the little strength left available to them in further attempts to re-establish contact. Rommel would have none of it and ordered further attacks to continue next day, an unfortunate decision for him which played straight into the hands of Montgomery.

The latter held an important conference at eight o'clock next morning, November 1st. Zero hour for 'Supercharge' was now fixed for five minutes past one that night. The infantry objectives were to be captured by a quarter to four. There would then be a pause of two hours, after which in the half light of dawn Currie's tanks would advance for 2,000 yards behind a barrage up to the Rahman track. Briggs' leading tanks would cross the existing front line at half past five and pass through Currie's on the line of the track at a quarter to seven. Lumsden was then to take over command of the battle with Bosvile on the right flank, Fisher in the centre and Custance on the left. The RAF were to concentrate on 21st Panzer and 90th Light Divisions and Lumsden was to have his tactical headquarters with Freyberg.

While this conference was in progress, the Afrika Korps, watched by Rommel, was preparing to renew its attempt to make contact with Thompson's Post. Godfrey's 24th Australian Brigade had relieved the 26th during the night and taken over command of 40th Royal Tanks, who now had 16 Valentines. A strong force of Stukas was intercepted by the RAF at half past eight and almost all were shot down before they could drop their bombs. This may have caused the attack to be postponed, as there was every sign of one being mounted shortly afterwards, but it did not develop until midday. The battle continued all afternoon, the Germans making repeated attempts to break through on the line of the road and railway, and 24th Brigade with the gallant Rhodesian 289th anti-tank battery beating off one attack after another, until at a quarter past five brigade headquarters received a direct hit, Godfrey himself being mortally wounded, three other senior officers killed and two wounded. It appears that at some time that day 24th Brigade was forced back south of the railway and that the Afrika Korps re-established contact with Thompson's Post and withdrew their forces during the night.

By that time however the centre of interest had shifted further south. Percy's 151st Brigade, the right hand brigade of the New Zealand Division attack, had been given 28th Maori Battalion and 8th Royal Tanks with 44 Valentines. The Maoris attacked on the right to form a right flank guard, eventually facing north. Their leading companies came under heavy fire soon after crossing the start line and their colonel was wounded. They had heavy casualties and companies lost touch with each other. All fought their way forward with the utmost gallantry, regardless of the fact that the tanks which were to support them never appeared. By dawn, now commanded by a captain, they were more or less where they were meant to be, having captured 162 German and 189 Italian prisoners and lost 33 killed and 75 wounded themselves. 8th Durham Light Infantry, attacking due west on the right, found the wait of nearly two hours in the forming up area cold, dressed as they were in shorts, shirts and cardigans. They moved off on time and reached their first objective at half past two as planned, but the two leading companies were severely reduced by about 100 casualties and only had 3 officers left between them. The reserve company pushed on and reached the final objective with little difficulty by four o'clock, capturing 50 Italians on the way.

On their left 9th Durham Light Infantry had very little trouble and were on their final objectives at the same time with only 30 casualties. 6th Durham Light Infantry followed up the 8th and came in on the right flank between them and the Maoris, having been engaged with elements of both 15th Panzer Division and Littorio on the way and lost 7 officers and 78 men. 8th Royal Tanks had been held up for a time by the usual mine-clearing difficulties, but were with the infantry of the brigade on its objectives before dawn.

The left brigade of the attack was Murray's 152nd from the Highland Division. As a means of recognising each other at night, they carried a white cross of St Andrew on their backs, formed by fixing strips of 'four by two' rifle-cleaning flannel to the braces of their web equipment. On the right 5th Seaforth reached their final objectives easily by a quarter to four, although two company commanders were wounded. 5th Camerons on the left had a tougher fight, and had great difficulty in maintaining direction and keeping touch with each other. However they completed their task on time, but were troubled by enemy tanks at dawn, their anti-tank guns not reaching them until nine o'clock. Before then the Valentines of 50th Royal Tanks had joined them, and the attention of enemy tanks had been fully engaged by Currie's advance.

Freyberg had agreed to this being postponed from a quarter to to a quarter past six, owing to delays in the move forward and doubts about actual progress. 3rd Hussars had been shelled on the way up and 12 of their tanks had fallen out for one reason or another, leaving them with 11 Shermans, 7 Grants and 5 Crusaders. They reached the forward positions of 9th Durham Light Infantry at a quarter past five. The Royal Wiltshire Yeomanry reached their position in the centre a quarter of an hour later, and the Warwickshire Yeomanry the front of Murray's Brigade at a quarter to six, having lost six tanks on mines on the way. All three regiments had found it difficult to find their way forward in the darkness and thick dust.

3rd Hussars set off badly, as one of the heavy squadrons was disorganised by the commander's tank going up on a mine, the wireless of the tank to which he transferred being 'off net' and one complete troop being missing when they started. 'A' Squadron had only three Crusaders with which to lead the advance. Fortunately there was little opposition at first and an encouraging number of prisoners. The regiment was reduced to only seven tanks when it reached the Rahman track, but by that time the Bays had caught up with them.

The Royal Wiltshire crossed the start line with 8 Shermans, 10 Grants and 15 Crusaders, 11 tanks having fallen out on the way. Their Crusader squadron led the way and, on reaching its final position just before first light, found itself on top of a large number of anti-tank guns which opened fire from all directions. Its only hope was to charge, which it did, and then turned south where some enemy tanks were reported. The squadron commander's tank was knocked out and the rest of the regiment knew no more of what had happened. By then the heavy squadrons were under fire, the barrage was going well ahead and the gunner O.P. officer could not be found. The regiment fired smoke and the anti-tank fire eased off a bit. Most of it had come from the tanks on the left, which had at first been mistaken for the Warwickshires. The regiment was told to hang on at all costs until 1st Armoured Division came up.

The Warwickshire Yeomanry, who had crossed the start line with 38 tanks, had a very similar experience. They were told to fight it out until the armoured division arrived, and then got involved in a confused action firing in all directions.

Meanwhile Freyberg had been doing all he could to get Briggs to hurry on. He rang up Leese at twenty-five minutes to eight and told him that Currie had had very heavy casualties and was 'very thin on the ground'. He said that Fisher was moving forward very slowly and asked that he should be hurried up.

Leese agreed to speak to Lumsden. Three minutes later Freyberg rang up again to repeat his urgent request. Before a further ten minutes had passed, he rang once more to say that he now believed that they had at last reached the forward infantry positions, but that enemy tanks were closing in from the north and he was afraid of a stalemate. He thought that the impetus was diminishing and that a senior officer of 10th Corps should be in the forward area to urge them on. Half an hour later Currie was still urging Freyberg to get Fisher forward, as his regiments, particularly the Royal Wiltshires, were in a desperate situation.

All three of Fisher's regiments, the Bays on the right, 9th Lancers in the centre and 10th Hussars on the left, were in fact now in action, although they were still behind Currie's few remaining tanks. They had started off from their assembly area at half past two that morning and had spent the night grinding forward slowly, enveloped in clouds of dust in pitch darkness, along tracks congested with masses of vehicles which should have been cleared off. To make matters worse 10th Hussars had taken a wrong turning and had to turn round and come back. Currie complained that Fisher was preoccupied with deploying into battle formation instead of coming to his aid. In fact Fisher's tanks were not as far west as they were meant to be, and it was not a simple task to deploy from three lanes in an area which was occupied by the infantry and in which Currie's tanks were being severely shot up by enemy tanks and anti-tank guns, well sited on the ridge behind the track to the west. The area was grossly congested, wreathed in smoke from burning tanks and from the artillery fire of both sides, which added to the dust churned up by tank tracks.

Soon after 30th Corps had issued a warning that attacks were to be expected by 21st Panzer from the north and 15th from the west, Freyberg again spoke to Leese at ten o'clock, saying that the situation was still unsatisfactory as the reinforcing armour had not moved up and the tanks that were in front were stationary. In fact at that very time the Bays on the right were just coming up level with 3rd Hussars, and 8th Royal Tanks also were on their right flank. Forty minutes later it was acknowledged that Fisher's tanks were now

through the battered remnants of Currie's. The latter had
lost 70 tanks that morning, the Royal Wiltshire reduced to 2,
50 men and 11 of their officers casualties, including Gibb,
their colonel, and all three squadron leaders wounded. 3rd
Hussars were down to 8 tanks, although they had only
lost 15. They appear to have had about the same number of
casualties, and the Warwickshire, with a loss of 24, were
reduced at that time to 7: their casualties were 26.

Currie and Freyberg both said that a vigorous push would
carry Fisher through the anti-tank screen beyond the track.
But in fact the position was now much stronger than it had
been four hours earlier when Currie had tried just that, failed
and lost heavily in the process.

The Panzer Armee had chosen this night to change back
from German Summer Time to Central European Time.
This cannot have helped matters, and their chances of avoiding confusion were greatly diminished when a heavy air
attack hit the advanced battle headquarters of Afrika Korps,
slightly wounding von Thoma. Telephone communication
was not restored until half past five and Rommel could only
get messages to the main headquarters. At first they thought
that the attack had been made further north than was the
case. They imagined it to have been a thrust west from the
Australian position to the south-east of Sidi Abd el Rahman.
By four o'clock they knew of the attack further south which
had driven in the left flank of 15th Panzer Division, but
still thought that this was a second thrust. At a quarter to
five orders were given for both Panzer divisions to attack
immediately, the 21st to move north towards Sidi Abd el
Rahman and then east to deal with the supposed northern
thrust. By first light Afrika Korps realised the true situation, although the details of it were still very obscure. They
were out of touch with von Randow, and got a message
relayed through Panzer Armee to stop the 21st. Von Sponeck
with his 90th Light Division was now directly under Rommel
to free von Thoma to command the counter-attack. The
latter joined von Vaerst at 15th Panzer Division's headquarters, arriving there at a quarter past eight. He then
arranged for the 21st to attack the salient from the north while

the 15th, collecting also the available Italian tanks of Littorio and Trieste, was to attack at the same time from the west. He could not get this going until eleven, which almost coincided with the final emergence of 2nd Armoured Brigade.

Montgomery was aware of the confusion existing 'on the other side of the hill'. He left his headquarters at half past seven for Leese's tactical headquarters, now south-west of Tel el Eisa. The picture painted to him was an encouraging one. 30th Corps had reached all their objectives. Their right flank, which faced the main strength of Rommel's forces, was secure. It was clear that 10th Corps' plan to push due west was already meeting considerable opposition which, if anything, was growing, although no counter-attack had yet developed. The southern flank appeared to be an area of promising development. The Royals had got two squadrons of armoured cars right out into the open desert this way, and the opposition in this sector seemed to be considerably weaker. One of the squadron leaders described their break-out to a war correspondent in these words:

We left our location and passed through the minefields in single file. No shot was fired at us. The only impediment to our progress occurred when the first car ran into an 88-mm. gun-pit filled with German dead. One or two more cars, including three petrol replenishing lorries, got stuck in slit trenches, but most of them pulled out when dawn broke and fought their way up to us. The enemy was too astounded to do anything as we came through, or else the Italian sections thought we were Germans, and the German section thought we were Italians. They waved swastika flags at us with vigour and we replied with 'Achtung!' and anything else we could think of which, with an answering wave, would get us through their lines. As it grew lighter they stared and blinked at us. Although a warning artillery barrage had been going on all night they couldn't believe their eyes. They would goggle at us from short range, see our berets, bolt away a few yards, pause as if they didn't think it was true, and come back to take another look.

We passed within 10 yards of the muzzles of an entire

battery of field artillery. Right down the columns we went with Germans standing by their guns, and, fortunately, failing to let them go off. One of them would suddenly see we were British, and run a few yards to tell someone else. Then both of them would stare unbelievingly.

As the dawn broke, we passed a man in bed. From the mass of vehicles and equipment surrounding him, he was obviously an Italian quarter-master. We woke him up by tossing a Verey light into his blankets. He broke the record for the sitting high jump. Into one of his lorries we heaved a hand-grenade. The results on the lorry were most satisfactory, but it scared the second-in-command who, following in his armoured car, had failed to see us toss the grenade.

Picking our way through trenches and gun positions we came upon what was evidently a permanent headquarters. Lorries were dug in and men were asleep everywhere. They were surprised to wake up and see their lorries go up in smoke one by one. We were now some miles behind their lines and their astonishment had been so colossal that we hadn't had one shot fired at us. It was full daylight and, getting among the soft transport vehicles, our work of destruction began. In the first quarter of an hour the two squadrons destroyed 40 lorries, simply by putting a bullet through the petrol tank and setting a match to the leak. The crews of lorries which had got bogged in the breakthrough, transferred themselves to German vehicles holding petrol. Spare men climbed aboard Italian vehicles mounted with Breda guns, and on we pushed. Germans panicked from their lorries into slit trenches. We had no time to take prisoners. We just took their weapons and told them to start walking east. Only those who refused were shot. Few refused. . . . The majority were most anxious to oblige us in every way, and readily assisted in draining vehicles we thought fit to immobilise. The Italians asked for greater consideration. We explained we couldn't take them all, and, skimming off the cream, pushed on with a colonel and two majors clinging for dear life round the muzzles of our 2-pounders.

Montgomery decided to take advantage of the weakness

which had been revealed in the south. As far as Lumsden was concerned, he decided that Custance should disregard enemy pressure from the north and move south-westwards round Fisher's southern flank instead of waiting to follow through him. Orders to this effect were given to the brigade soon after half past ten. That afternoon 30th Corps were to attack 'Skinflint', or Point 38, a slight rise a mile south-west of 2nd Seaforth's new position on the right of Murray's Brigade, and they were to be given 5th Indian Brigade as a further infantry reserve after its relief that night. In order to exploit the success he hoped for, Harding was to be moved forward as soon as possible under Lumsden's command, and would probably be pushed through the southern flank of the salient and directed on Ghazal Station, eight miles west of Sidi Abd el Rahman. Roddick was to move up north and also join Lumsden. His brigade would probably be used to exploit a second gap which might be made further south the following night. Having made these decisions, Montgomery returned to his own headquarters at mid-day.

Meanwhile the battle raged fast and furious astride the Rahman track. Fisher found progress impossible as his tanks were continually engaged with enemy tanks and anti-tank guns, principally from the north and north-west, accompanied by constant artillery fire. It was the fiercest and most prolonged tank engagement of the whole battle. For nearly two hours, from eleven until one, the Afrika Korps attempted to drive 2nd Armoured Brigade back. The latter, almost stationary the whole time, kept up a constant fire from their tank guns, and were supported by a great weight of artillery and at least seven attacks by the familiar formations of 18 light bombers. Rommel sacrificed his anti-aircraft protection to his need for anti-tank guns and brought up every 88-mm. gun within reach, giving him a total of 24 before they began to be knocked out. The Italian tanks suffered particularly heavily and their officers could no longer keep them in the line. Von Thoma and Rommel realised in the early afternoon that their first counter-attack had failed. Ordering the Afrika Korps to attack again at two o'clock, Rommel decided to bring north the main part of Ariete, still down in the south, with a large part of the artillery in that area, thus denuding the southern sector of practically all reserves. He also decided that the time had come for him to shorten his front in the coastal sector and pull it back to Sidi abd el Rahman.

While Fisher and von Thoma continued to batter away at each other, attempts were made to push Custance out to the south-west. It took some time to extricate his tanks from their involvement in dealing with 15th Panzer Division's attacks. When at mid-day they eventually began to emerge, they soon came up against the usual anti-tank screen and made no further progress all day, having lost 6 Crusaders and claiming to have knocked out 11 enemy tanks. To their left rear Wimberley was preparing his attack on 'Skinflint', to be carried out by 2nd Seaforth and 50th Royal Tanks, supported by a considerable artillery programme. Zero hour, originally fixed for four o'clock, was altered to six, then to six-thirty and back again to quarter past, thoroughly confusing the gunners. However all went like clockwork, the infantry had no casualties, the tanks lost 4 Valentines, two on mines and two from gunfire, and 100 prisoners were taken from Trieste, who were so shaken that they also surrendered 'Snipe' with a further 60 prisoners before Lee's 5th Royal Sussex had even had time to attack it.

Von Thoma, having failed to make any impression in his second attack in the afternoon, ordered yet another to be made by Panzer Grenadiers of the 21st on the northern flank of the salient at last light; but it does not seem ever in fact to have been delivered. The Afrika Korps was now down to 35 serviceable tanks and had fired off a great deal of the remaining stock of ammunition. Rommel took the fateful decision to withdraw to Fuka, 60 miles further back, pulling out his troops in the southern sector during the night to the old line from Qaret el Abd to Gebel Kalakh. In the north his mobile forces, Afrika Korps, XX Corps and 90th Light Division were to resist 8th Army's pressure, withdrawing slowly next day to a line running south from Daba, 20 miles back, while the infantry got away on foot or on whatever vehicles could be made available.

Rommel reported his decision to Hitler's headquarters, saying that his army was now exhausted physically and materially and could no longer expect to prevent a break-through, which he saw as inevitable next day. He could not hope to disengage and would rescue what he could, but his shortage both of vehicles and of petrol severely limited what he could achieve. His nightly letter to his wife had a fatalistic ring and could not have been cheering to receive:

3 Nov. 1942.

Dearest Lu,

The battle is going very heavily against us. We're simply being crushed by the enemy weight. I've made an attempt to salvage part of the army. I wonder if it will succeed. At night I lie open-eyed, racking my brains for a way out of this plight for my poor troops.

We are facing very difficult days, perhaps the most difficult that a man can undergo. The dead are lucky, it's all over for them. I think of you constantly with heartfelt love and gratitude. Perhaps all will be well and we shall see each other again.

11 BREAK AWAY

November 3rd – 7th

By last light on November 2nd Briggs had made no progress, but claimed, probably correctly, to have knocked out 62 enemy tanks for the loss of only 10 of his own, all but two from the Bays on the right. Casualties had been extremely light and Fisher still mustered over 100 tanks, Custance adding another 86. Harding was now close behind with at least as many more in Roberts' brigade.

Lumsden's plan was for Fisher and Custance to advance westwards for five miles during the night, while Bosvile was to turn southwards across the Rahman track, Harding then moving forward at first light. This was changed, probably at Montgomery's instigation, for a less ambitious plan. Bosvile was to attack that night and capture the area north of Tel el Aqqaqir which had been Briggs' objective for that day. If he succeeded, Fisher and Custance were to pass through, followed later in the morning by Harding. A further attempt was made to get the rest of the Royals and 4th South African Armoured Car Regiment out as well. A complicated series of regroupings was also to be initiated in 30th Corps, designed to free the New Zealanders and make more infantry available for attack.

This late change gave the unfortunate 7th Motor Brigade little time to prepare their attack, due to start at a quarter past one that night. As a result a very scrappy plan was made with little artillery support, each battalion being left more or less to make its own separate plan. 2nd Rifle Brigade were given a most ambitious task, having to advance a mile west from where the 9th Lancers had spent the day to the Rahman track and yet another mile beyond. On the left 2nd/60th were to capture Tel el Aqqaqir itself, advancing 2,000 yards westwards from the south-west corner of the salient held by Murray's brigade. In the centre, 7th Rifle Brigade were to advance to the track itself, no artillery support being planned on the mistaken assumption that their task only involved reoccupying an area which had been held by another unit during the day.

2nd Rifle Brigade soon found themselves embroiled with a strong enemy position astride the track. Their anti-tank guns could not get forward and they were reduced to 60 men on the objective, 7 officers being casualties. The ground was too hard for digging and a great many enemy had come to life behind them. Pearson therefore sought and obtained permission to withdraw to the start line. Much the same experience befell their sister battalion, the 7th. Far from a peaceful occupation, they found themselves hotly engaged on the track itself and soon reduced in strength. The situation remained confused for some time, but finally also resulted in a withdrawal to the start line. On the left 2nd/60th had a bad start, as a mistake in the transmission of a signal led them to believe that zero hour had been postponed for an hour. They were therefore surprised when the artillery programme started on time and naturally found themselves a long way behind it. In any case their depleted strength had left them with only two motor companies. They could get no closer than 500 yards to the track and dug in there, only to find themselves at dawn completely overlooked by the high ground of Tel el Aqqaqir itself, uncomfortably close. Unfortunately Briggs was under the impression that they had captured it, a misconception which persisted for some twelve hours and had an unfortunate effect on the events of the day.

In this belief, but realising that both the other two battalions had failed, Lumsden ordered Briggs to send Fisher forward to join the 60th round Tel el Aqqaqir, while Custance, instead of passing through would again attempt to push out to the south of him. Both brigades crept cautiously forward at first light, but neither made any progress. They both fired very large quantities of ammunition against enemy anti-tank guns on the slight ridge beyond the track, and did in fact destroy a great number of them. Very few casualties were incurred, even when in the early afternoon the Sherwood Rangers on Custance's extreme left made an unsuccessful attempt to rush the ridge. They lost only one tank themselves, but the Staffordshire Yeomanry, supporting them

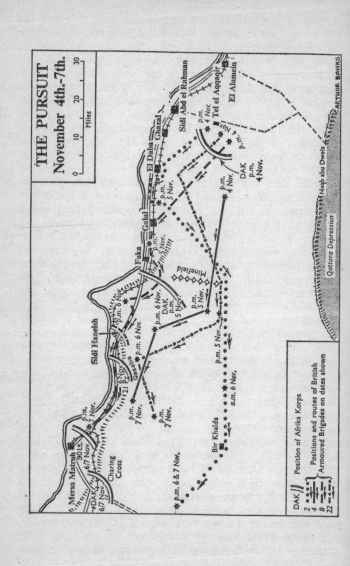

THE PURSUIT
November 4th.-7th.

0   10   20   30
Miles

DAK // Position of Afrika Korps

Positions and routes of British
Armoured Brigades on dates shown

2
4
8
22

ARTHUR BANKS

on the right, lost three. The only result of this well-intentioned action was unfortunate, in that it led to a false report that they had succeeded in establishing themselves west of the track.

Montgomery had summoned his Corps Commanders at a quarter past nine. He already sensed that Rommel was at his last gasp and looked to the southern side of the salient as the most promising for a break-through. While they were in conference, reports arrived of explosions on the front of 13th Corps and of enemy withdrawing in that sector. These, coupled with the falsely optimistic reports of the progress of 10th Corps, presented a picture of relaxed resistance on the whole front. Montgomery decided that Wimberley, reinforced by 5th Indian Brigade, was to carry out a further deep attack south-westwards that night, and that yet another attempt was to be made to get the armoured cars out.

At the opposing Army Headquarters the cold light of dawn made Rommel realise that the report he had sent the night before might not be fully appreciated by his masters. He therefore decided to send his ADC, Lieutenant Berndt, to report direct to Hitler. He was to press for the fullest freedom of action and explain Rommel's plan to fight a succession of rearguard actions until either he was reinforced sufficiently to defeat his opponent or, if not, he could successfully evacuate his army across the Mediterranean. Having done this, he set off along the coast road to his forward headquarters, surprised that the RAF were not already attacking the transport, mostly Italian, already jammed along it.

On arrival he got in touch with von Thoma and Bayerlein and was told that 8th Army were not making any serious attempt to attack the Afrika Korps, who still had only 30 tanks; but their units seemed to be engaged in reorganising and replenishing, confining their activities to local probing attacks. Rommel, relieved and surprised, decided to take the opportunity of this lull to order most of the Italians to start their withdrawal. This soon added to the congestion on the coast road and it was not long before the RAF took advantage of it. When Rommel set off back to his main headquarters, he only just missed being caught in one of these attacks himself. Soon after his return, at half past one by his time, which was now half past three by 8th Army time, Hitler's reply to his report of the previous night arrived:

To Field-Marshal Rommel

It is with trusting confidence in your leadership and the courage of the German-Italian troops under your command that the German people and I are following the heroic struggle in Egypt. In the situation in which you find yourself there can be no other thought but to stand fast, yield not a yard of ground and throw every gun and every man into the battle. Considerable air force reinforcements are being sent to C-in-C South. The Duce and the Comando Supremo are also making the utmost efforts to send you the means to continue the fight. Your enemy, despite his superiority, must also be at the end of his strength. It would not be the first time in history that a strong will has triumphed over the bigger battalions. As to your troops, you can show them no other road than that to victory or death.

It was a stunning blow. In a mood of fatalistic apathy orders for withdrawal were cancelled. These were not easy to put into effect, particularly in X Corps sector in the south which was already in difficulties as a result of the activities of the Royals behind its front. Berndt had not yet left, but went off that evening with a message that, if Hitler's orders were upheld, the final destruction of the Panzer Armee was a matter of a few days only and that it had already caused 'immense harm'. One cannot but sympathise with poor Berndt in his thankless mission.

While the Panzer Armee were trying to reverse their withdrawal, Wimberley was preparing the blow which was to lead to the final break-out. The first step was to be an attack by 5th/7th Gordons and 8th Royal Tanks just before last light south-westwards from 'Skinflint' to the track two miles south of Tel el Aqqaqir. At half past one in the morning Russell's 5th Indian Brigade was to start an attack from the eastern part of 'Skinflint' which, after an advance of four miles, would bring them to the track three miles south of the Gordons. Finally at dawn 7th Argylls would take Tel el Aqqaqir

The first attack was to have been preceded by an intensive air attack on the track itself and supported by a considerable weight of artillery. When Briggs got to hear of it, he moved heaven and earth to get both stopped, thinking it would fall on the 60th and 8th Armoured Brigade, being still under a false impression of the progress both had made. In fact the air attack would certainly have been uncomfortably close to the latter, whose southern regiment might also just have been touched by the edge of the artillery programme. The picture he gave Wimberley of their dispositions was however a false one and led the latter to tell the attacking troops to make a last-minute change in plan to an unopposed and unsupported advance, carrying infantry on the leading tanks, who were sceptical about the basis of the change. For the first twenty minutes all went well, but then as the smoke cleared intense anti-tank and machine gun fire was met. The infantry were swept off the tanks which continued to press forward towards the setting sun, unable to locate the flashes of the anti-tank guns. 20 tanks were lost with 27 casualties, 7 being officers. The Gordons, having had over 90 casualties, dug in only 1,000 yards beyond the Seaforths, the 12 remaining tanks rallying behind them.

The preliminaries to Russell's attack augured no better. It was mid-day before the brigade got its orders at a conference at Leese's tactical headquarters. Fortunately the Commanders of the Corps and New Zealand Divisional Artillery were there and an extensive but simple artillery programme was laid on, in which nine field regiments were to fire a total of 37,200 rounds and two medium regiments, which alone could reach the final objective, would fire 4,352.

The battalions had a long journey to make to reach the start line. The colonel of 1st/4th Essex, who was to lead on the right, found his unit after his reconnaissance and gave them their orders at a quarter past seven. 3rd/10th Baluchs were to lead on the left, but their commanding officer could not find them anywhere. 6th Rajputana Rifles were to have been in reserve. Half an hour before midnight, when it was clear that the Baluchs were still missing, their unfortunate colonel, who himself had only been able to assemble half his battalion, was told to take their place on the left. Zero hour could not be postponed for more than an hour if they were to reach their objective by dawn. At half past two therefore the attack began and went like clockwork, in spite of considerable trouble caused by extensive patches of soft sand.

The Essex picked up 100 prisoners from von Vaerst's Panzer Grenadier Regiment on the way and 80 more on their objective, which they reached ahead of time at ten past seven. The other two battalions met practically no opposition. The Rajputana Rifles got there on time, their missing companies not joining them until the afternoon, and the Baluchs, found at last, got there also by nine o'clock. At first light 7th Argylls took Tel el Aqqaqir without a fight. Under cover of the distraction caused by Rommel's attack, the rest of the Royals and 4th South African Armoured Cars slipped out to the south and then turned west.

Rommel appears to have been ignorant of these events and under the impression that Montgomery had made no move. He had withdrawn the Afrika Corps six miles north-west during the night, bringing 90th Light Division back to the area of Ghazal station on the left. On the right was de Stefanis' XX Corps, in fact Ariete with the remnants of Littorio and Trieste attached to it, and south of them again Trento, Ramcke and X Corps, or what was left of them, now commanded by General Nobbia, in place of Orsi, who had been killed a few days before the battle began. Rommel had had a bad night, a mass of vehicles on the coast road alongside his headquarters having been attacked ceaselessly all night and many of them abandoned. Kesselring arrived to see him in the early morning and met with a hot reception. Rommel imagined that Hitler's orders had been based on optimistic reports sent back by the Luftwaffe, and vented his wrath accordingly on his unfortunate superior, who was ill-advised as to suggest that the order was based on the experience Hitler had gained from events on the Russian front. Still seething with anger, Rommel set off to visit von Thoma's main headquarters.

The previous evening Montgomery had given his orders for the final break-out which he saw was imminent. In 30th Corps the Australians were to clear up the area of 'the pocket' east of Sidi Abd el Rahman. Freyberg, reinforced by Roddick, was to break out as soon as possible and make for Sidi Ibeid, ten miles south-west of Russell's objective, prepared to move immediately to block Rommel's retreat at Fuka, 45 miles to the north-west. Wimberley was to be prepared to relieve him at Sidi Ibeid. Lumsden's main task was to operate northwards and clear up the coastal sector. Briggs was to pivot on Tel el Aqqaqir and aim at occupying the area three miles SSE of Ghazal station, while Harding, passing round his southern flank, was directed to Ghazal station itself, where he was to cut the coast road. The RAF were to concentrate all their efforts on the road immediately west of the front during the night and westwards from Daba during the day. Arrangments were to be put in hand at once to implement 'Operation Grapeshot'. Gairdner's headquarters of 8th Armoured Division with 68 Valentines of 23rd Armoured Brigade on light tank tranporters, 5th RHA, a lorried infantry battalion and a machine gun battalion, sappers, light anti-aircraft and anti-tank gunners, was to assemble south of Ghazal station as soon as practicable. Accompanied by a large RAF party of 160 vehicles and taking over command of the two armoured car regiments already operating in Rommel's rear, this force was to make straight for Tobruk in order to seize it before the enemy could organise its defence. Part of the force was to be dropped off on the way to hold an intermediate airfield, preferably near Sidi Barrani. The problem was to decide whether it was to move along the coast road or through the desert. If the latter, heavy transporters would be needed and speed much reduced. The decision would be taken when the force was finally assembled at Ghazal, ready to move, it was hoped, early in the morning of the 5th.

Lumsden's original plan had been for Harding to lead the way by breaking out to the south-west during the night, keeping clear of Wimberley's attack. Briggs was to follow soon after first light, passing to the south of Tel el Aqqaqir and then turning north-west. He would then either help Harding if necessary or go straight on to Fuka. Custance would be dropped off to join Gatehouse, who was to be prepared to follow Briggs as soon as his artillery was freed from supporting Wimberley. In the middle of the night these orders were changed to conform to those given by Montgomery, Briggs being given the rather vague task of 'advancing to outflank the enemy'. In this revised plan Custance, coming under Gatehouse, was to advance on the left of Briggs and fill the gap between him and Harding.

Acting on these orders, Fisher broke leaguer at first light, but did not move forward at once because of the early morning mist. This cleared at a quarter to eight and the brigade advanced cautiously, led by the armoured cars of 12th Lancers and closely followed by Briggs himself, whose tank was hit and put out of action at ten o'clock, when the brigade's tanks came up against the Afrika Korps' rear-guard position. 21st Panzer Division held a line running east and west three miles north-west of Tel el Aqqaqir, its right flank joining the left flank of 15th Panzer, whose line ran south from there. Fisher's advance led straight at this junction point and, as pressure increased, von Thoma brought his *Kampfstaffel* into the line. By mid-day the German position was getting precarious as more and more of their tanks and anti-tank guns were knocked out and the *Kampfstaffel* itself was destroyed in trying to hold Tel el Mampsra, the key to the centre of the position. Von Thoma's own tank was knocked out and he surrendered to Captain Grant Singer, Commander of the 10th Hussars Reconnaissance Troop, while Bayerlein made his escape on foot, reaching his main headquarters two hours later, where he reported to Rommel. Von Thoma dined with Montgomery that night and expressed the hope that Rommel would make yet another come-back from Agheila.

The latter was now equally concerned at the news coming from the right where enormous dust clouds could be seen to the south and south-east. Westphal told Rommel on the telephone that the British had completely broken through the main defences in the centre. News also came from de Stefanis that his XX Corps was under heavy pressure from 100 or more British heavy tanks which had come round his right flank.

The former threat came from Roddick with the New Zealanders and the latter from Harding. His 'Desert Rats' had begun to move forward soon after five the evening before and leaguered in the salient area at eight, remaining in march formation. They were to move forward again at a quarter to three to pass through 5th Indian Brigade, but this was twice postponed to allow the latter to complete their task. At half past six the advance began with 11th Hussars leading, but the heavy mist and soft sand slowed it down, so that it was half past eight before they passed through Russell's brigade. Soon after a large enemy column was sighted, to which Roberts gave chase. Harding told him not to get delayed by a force which only seemed to have about a dozen Italian tanks with it, but to thrust it aside or pass round it. A period of confused fighting followed, in which Roberts tried to leapfrog his regiments successively to the left. Resistance continued to be stubborn, anti-tank fire including 88-mm. At one o'clock the opposition slackened and Roberts turned south a bit before making west again. Six miles further on more tanks and guns were met and the battle was resumed. It went on until dark, by which time Ariete, to whose gallantry Rommel paid tribute, was completely encircled and totally destroyed. Roberts' brigade had destroyed 29 Italian tanks and taken 450 prisoners losing only one light tank of its own and having practically no casualties.

At the same time the Royal Scots Greys with Roddick were completing the destruction of an Italian battery a few miles to the south. Their brigade had been right back north of El Alamein station the previous afternoon. To reach their start line, in order to lead the advance of the New Zealand Division at dawn, they had to cross the lines of advance of both 1st and 7th Armoured Divisions and assemble in the same area as the 10th. Little if any attempt seems to have been made on a higher level to co-ordinate the confusion that was bound to arise from so many divisions struggling to push out through the bottleneck of the salient area. It would have been hard enough if all had been under the command of the same corps; with two different corps, who were not on the best of terms anyway, both trying to carry out the same task in the same area, it was chaotic. There is no other word to describe the incredible confusion of that dark night in a sea of dust. Vehicles of every formation were travelling in every direction on every conceivable track, looming up in front of each other from unexpected directions out of the thick, stifling pall of dust. It is not surprising that the brigade fell four hours behind programme and its leading armoured cars, 2nd Derbyshire Yeomanry, did not reach Tel el Aqqaqir until a quarter past eight. They halted there for two hours, while Freyberg attempted to find a route which did not coincide with or cross that being taken by somebody else. By this time Roberts' brigade were all west of the Rahman track; Roddick then set off southwards and turned west to cross the track at one o'clock two miles south of where Roberts had done so. By edging southwards again he managed to avoid the battle going on to the north and made good progress until last light, when he leaguered 15 miles on, the same distance south of Daba. The Greys joined him at midnight after their successful battle on the right flank which accounted for 11 guns and 300 prisoners. The rest of Freyberg's division was however still strung out behind all the way back to its starting point.

Another formation had now joined in what might be called the 'left hook game'. At mid-day Lumsden realised that Fisher was clearly up against fairly strong opposition. Roberts was already quite close to his left flank and there was little to be gained from pushing Custance between the two. The 8th had been stationary near Tel el Aqqaqir since dawn and Custance was now ordered to form up on the track facing south and then move off to the south-west. He was to move round Harding's flank during the night and make for Daba by dawn, thus adding to the criss-cross pattern of movement. He did not get going until half past four, his assembly being delayed by a Stuka attack, and halted at last light three miles west of the track, two miles south-east of Roberts and ten miles east of Roddick, only a mile from where the Greys were finishing off the Italian battery.

That evening Rommel realised clearly that he was in danger of encirclement by an enemy with twenty times as many tanks. There was no longer any point in attempting to obey his Fuhrer's orders. After discussing the situation with Bayerlein, who had now taken over command of the Afrika Korps, he gave the order at half past five (8th Army time) for the retreat to begin immediately. It was to be 'sauve qui peut' and it was clear that only the motorised forces stood any chance. Every vehicle that could do so made for the road and away.

Montgomery hoped to catch the Panzer Armee before it could escape. His plan was for Freyberg to continue to Fuka and for Custance to be directed on Galal, between Fuka and Daba, both during the night. Briggs and Harding were not to move. These orders were modified during the night when the RAF reported that there was a solid mass of vehicles all the way from Daba to Fuka, and Lumsden was urged to push on boldly and get the Royals and 4th South African Armoured Cars to delay the enemy at the Fuka escarpment.

In fact neither Freyberg nor Custance were moving. Kippenberger's brigade was now up with Roddick and Freyberg had intended to set off again at eleven that night, but Gentry's 6th Brigade and the rest of the division were still a long way back. Their start had been delayed by the fearful confusion and congestion in the original salient area and some did not begin to move until it was nearly dark. Night movement in a strange desert, through which parties of the enemy were still also attempting to move, was a slow business. Freyberg's determination to collect the division before starting was reinforced by a message from 30th Corps that 15th Panzer Division was also heading for Fuka. After two postponements the start was eventually fixed for half past five.

Custance had refuelled at last light and resumed his advance in pitch darkness at half past seven. So great was the confusion and difficulty in keeping touch caused by this, the first attempt of most of them at a night move over unreconnoitred desert, that he halted after an hour and decided not to try again until it was light. This does not seem to have been known higher up for a considerable time afterwards.

10th Corps issued a number of orders during the night. Lumsden's first plan was for Briggs to stay where he was at first light, while Harding made for the high ground west of Ghazal station and south-east of Daba. Custance was to make

for Galal between Daba and Fuka, while the rest of 10th
Armoured Division would be directed just south of Daba,
edging to the west if strong opposition were met.

At a quarter past five in the morning these orders were
changed. Gatehouse was to move as quickly as possible to
where the road climbed the escarpment just west of Fuka,
Custance joining him there as soon as he could. Briggs was
now to move directly on Daba while Harding on his left
was to cut the road and railway a few miles to the west. The
Royals and 4th South Africans, now joined by 3rd South
African Armoured Cars, were to concentrate on trying to
block the road up the Fuka escarpment. Later in the day
the New Zealanders would be transferred to 10th from 30th
Corps, and were now, at the request of the RAF, to be told
to capture the landing grounds near Sidi Haneish between
10 and 20 miles west of Fuka.

It was on these orders that divisions began to act at dawn.
Fisher set off at half past seven, led by 12th Lancers, and met
no opposition until a single 88-mm. opened fire three miles
south-east of Daba at nine o'clock, killing Captain Grant
Singer, von Thoma's captor of the day before. The brigade
then skirted the southern edge of Daba and cut it off on the
west, while Bosvile's riflemen laid on an attack. By half
past twelve they had occupied the village, collecting 150
stragglers, Fisher's tanks pushing some enemy westward down
the road and halting to refuel at four o'clock 10 miles further
west. Roberts had advanced on their left, but had been halted
5 miles south of Daba when it was clear that the enemy had
withdrawn.

Custance had started off at six, led by 'B' Squadron, 11th
Hussars. After a brush with a fair-sized enemy column flee-
ing west, they reached Galal without opposition and took
up a battle position astride the road and railway facing
east. Soon afterwards a column came along which was dealt
with by 3rd Royal Tanks. Just before mid-day enemy tanks
were seen to be approaching from the east. As they came
nearer more tanks, Italian M.13's, several guns and a larger
number of lorries were seen to be following. Unsuspecting
they made no attempt to deploy and ran headlong into the
devastating fire of the whole brigade. They were completely

destroyed and all was over within an hour; 29 Italian and 14 German tanks, 4 guns, 100 lorries and 1,000 prisoners were accounted for: 11 more tanks and many more vehicles were later found abandoned a little further south. This was a most satisfactory haul, and it is probable that it was all that remained of de Stefanis' XX Mobile Corps.

On the outside of the enveloping movement Roddick led off with the New Zealanders at six. Freyberg was aiming to pass 10 miles south of Fuka, where there was no escarpment, and then curve round right-handed to where the road west of Fuka came up on to the top of the escarpment. Twelve miles on and soon after dawn the Greys flushed a leaguer of 20 German tanks. Six of them were dealt with and the rest fled west. After a brush with a column moving across their front, the brigade were held up by a minefield running due south from Fuka, the one gap through it well covered by artillery fire. It was not until three o'clock that the first tanks were beyond it, and it was a slow process getting the rest of the brigade through.

By this time it was clear that Custance's brigade was the only one that had succeeded in cutting off any considerable body of the enemy. Montgomery was struggling through the tangled mass of traffic on his way up to see Lumsden when the RAF reported that a long column of vehicles stretched from four miles east of Fuka all the way to Matruh, 50 miles further west. It was clear that Freyberg and Gatehouse would be too late to catch them, and de Guingand got a message through to Montgomery by mid-day suggesting that Freyberg should immediately pass to Lumsden's command and be told to send his tanks and armoured cars straight to Charing Cross, where the road climbed the escarpment a few miles south-west of Matruh. He got no reply to this, Montgomery at the time being in conference with Lumsden. As a result of their discussion Lumsden sent new orders out by wireless at twenty minutes to two. Briggs was to be directed on Mersa Matruh, taking a wide sweep round through the desert by Bir Khalda, 40 miles south of his objective and 70 miles from where he then was near Daba. His division was to start at once and continue the move all through the night.

In a shorter hook, Harding was to capture the area of the landing grounds south of Sidi Haneish, between Fuka and Matruh, and cut the road north of them in three places. Gatehouse was to sweep up the area between Galal and Fuka, taking care not to fire on the New Zealanders or the armoured cars in that area. Lee took over Galal and Custance started westwards at half past three, but had covered less than 10 miles, half-way to Fuka, when he stopped to leaguer for the night. Harding had, in fact, already started his move some time before these new orders were issued, and by two o'clock Roberts was 12 miles south-east of Fuka, having to diverge to the south to clear the tail of the forward part of the New Zealand Division, engaged in their battle over the minefield. Turning west again Harding also ran into the minefield further south. 11th Hussars were still trying to find a way round, when armoured cars and sappers together proved it to be a dummy. It had in fact been laid by the British during the withdrawal in June. All this led to a delay of three hours and the advance did not get going again until six, being continued for another hour before halting for the night, which was in any case necessary for lack of petrol. The division had not that morning expected to be sent so far west. Petrol in the tanks was now low and the 'B echelons', which had delivered to them earlier in the day near Daba, had not themselves been replenished by the RASC by last light. When the tanks halted, 131st Lorried Infantry Brigade was hurrying along 15 miles behind, its units very scattered and their administrative situation somewhat disorganised.

Roberts was 20 miles SSW of Fuka and 25 miles south-east of his objectives. He was in fact only a few miles south-west of Roddick. The latter had been followed through the minefield, which the New Zealanders never discovered to be a dummy, by 5th New Zealand Brigade. Freyberg had originally intended to push Kippenberger on after dark to cut the coast road, but the delay caused by the opposition and the minefield led him to decide that they could not get there and dig in by dawn. He had also come to the conclusion that the enemy was holding the area north of him 'in strength' and might break out south-west during the night. Freyberg did not want to see a repetition of the events of June round Minqar Qaim, not far from where he now found himself again, and ordered Kippenberger to form a defensive position where he was, north-east of Roddick's tanks.

Rommel, whose headquarters south-west of Fuka was twice accurately bombed, had originally meant to make a stand at Fuka for as long as he could, while he got his infantry away. However, the appearance of Gatehouse west of Galal and the threat of outflanking, posed by the moves of Freyberg and Harding, forced him to order a further withdrawal to Matruh that night, realising that in doing so he was abandoning the bulk of the Italian infantry. His only effective fighting force was now 90th Light Division, the remnants of the Afrika Korps and a collection of other German army units. The coast road was a scene of wild confusion, vehicles jammed head to tail, many run out of fuel and either abandoned or on tow. Rommel managed to get his own headquarters, 15th Panzer and 90th Light back to the area of Charing Cross, south-west of Matruh. There was not enough petrol for 21st Panzer, who had to stay near Qasaba, south-west of Sidi Haneish, and a group based on 580 Reconnaissance Battalion, commanded by Captain Voss, one of Rommel's former ADC's, acted as rearguard west of Fuka.

In fact therefore the chance of forestalling Rommel at Charing Cross or cutting him off west of Fuka had gone, but all hopes were based on Briggs. His headquarters had been on the move when the new orders were received at two o'clock. 'At once' was given a liberal interpretation and a conference was held at Fisher's headquarters at twenty minutes to five, at which it was decided to start the move at six, 12th Lancers in the lead. The 'going' was bad, the night was very dark and there were a lot of old slit trenches about as well as a host of vehicles of other formations cutting across their path. Progress was slow, and by dawn 12th Lancers and Fisher's brigade were 15 miles east of Bir Khalda, having covered 55 miles in 12 hours. Briggs' headquarters was 8 miles further east and Bosvile's riflemen a further 15 miles behind. The advance was continued until nine, when it was brought to a stop by lack of petrol, the leading tanks still being well east of Bir Khalda. The 'B echelons' had been replenished by the divisional RASC the previous morning right back near Tel el Eisa, and had left that area at half past two in the afternoon, except for the echelon of the Bays, which had gone astray and did not leave the area until first light on the 6th. The echelons had got into great difficulties during the night march and did not reach the brigade until eleven in the morning, that of the Bays still being missing. Meanwhile the Divisional RASC, having filled itself up again, had set off in the late afternoon of the 5th to make the journey from El Alamein to Bir Khalda, hoping to arrive there early on the 6th, to replenish the 'B echelons', which were by then expected to have refuelled the tanks. They were delayed by the chaotic traffic congestion in the original battlefield area, and then struggled on through the night. Their route took them through an area of soft sand and the whole convoy got irretrievably stuck by three in the morning. It was useless to try and continue, and they waited till dawn before starting to dig themselves out.

At half past one, without the Bays, 2nd Armoured Brigade started off again, Colonel Roscoe Harvey, the second-in-command, replacing Fisher who had fallen ill. Briggs came along too, but by dark in the evening of the 6th they were still six miles from the Matruh-Siwa road and 20 miles from Charing Cross, where a large enemy force of 1,000 vehicles had been reported, when they ran out of petrol again. By this time the nearest supply was still in the hands of the RASC lorries nearly 80 miles behind which, having struggled out of the soft sand, now found themselves bogged down by rain as well.

While this tragedy of frustration was playing itself out, Harding was in action to the north-east. Roberts had set off again at first light and by ten o'clock 11th Hussars were reporting a considerable amount of traffic along the road. Half an hour later two columns appeared from the east, one after the other, probably the Voss group. The brigade just missed the tail of the first but knocked several feathers out of the second. The advance continued northward until petrol began to be a worry, 5th Royal Tanks being forced to halt.

However, the 'B echelons' caught up very soon afterwards and, while refuelling was in progress, 11th Hussars inspected landing grounds and tried to locate the main enemy force. At one o'clock this was reported to be on the edge of the escarpment a few miles west of the brigade. It was in fact 21st Panzer Division also out of fuel, although of course this was not known. Rain now began to fall heavily and, taking advantage of the reduced visibility Roberts advanced again at three and engaged the enemy, trying to work round their western flank as he did so. The action went on until dark when, destroying their few remaining tanks and guns, 21st Panzer managed to escape west to Charing Cross. By this time the skies had opened and rain was pouring down, turning the desert in this coastal area into a bog. Harding had been told early in the afternoon to set off as soon as he could on an outflanking move of 170 miles, through desert in which almost every stone was familiar, to catch the enemy as he climbed to the top of the escarpment on the frontier at Sollum and Halfaya. The weather effectively prevented any start being made on this long trek for the moment.

Further to the east Freyberg had been held up by lack of petrol until after mid-day, and then by rain, his principal action during the day being the repulse by Gentry at dawn of an attack on his rear, presumably by part of the retreating X Italian Corps. Gatehouse had spent the morning attacking the Fuka escarpment, and reached the top just before mid-day after an outflanking move, picking up 300 Italian prisoners. There he was visited by Montgomery and spent the rest of the day mopping up the area between Fuka and Galal, the torrential rain, which started in the afternoon and continued most of the night, making captors and captured alike fellows in sodden misery. In the morning he had been told to send all the petrol he could to Briggs, but it does not seem to have got there.

With everyone in the desert bogged down, all hope of progress now rested with a direct advance up the coast road, which Montgomery was desperately anxious to clear as far forward as possible in order to bring up both his 'tail' and the Royal Air Force. At half past two that night there-

fore, Gatehouse was told to push Custance's brigade along
the road to Matruh. They started off at half past six in the
morning of the 7th, attempting to move in desert formation
astride the road, but it took only 500 yards to prove that
this was impracticable. The next two and a half hours were
spent reorganising the brigade to move along the road, which
was already in use by all and sundry. It was not until mid-
day that the leading carrier and tanks reached the old Matruh
defences held by part of 90th Light, who opened fire. By this
time chaos and congestion blocked the road behind. An hour
and a half later 3rd Royal Tanks were told to work round
to the south of the defences, while the Sherwood Rangers
made a direct assault, led by their colonel, whose tank was
knocked out. Anti-tank fire also stopped the outflanking
move. There were no engineers and very few infantry available, Lee's brigade being still back at Galal and both they
and the motor battalion, 1st Buffs, having become almost
entirely absorbed in guarding and shepherding prisoners. In
any case 8th Armoured Brigade, where Gatehouse was also
himself, was out of wireless touch with both divisional headquarters and 133rd Brigade. Montgomery himself appeared
and 'seemed anxious to get to Matruh', presumably a masterly
understatement of his state of mind. Colonel Smith-Dorrien
of the Buffs carried out an attack all on his own at four,
which removed the road block and penetrated for 150 yards
without finding any mines; but when he tried again with one
platoon and a party of sappers that he had collected, they
were fired on at close range and driven back. A gap was not
finally cleared, making it possible to resume the advance,
until shortly before dawn next day, November 8th, by which
time the Germans had withdrawn.

Freyberg and Briggs had been bogged down all day,
although an attempt had been made to push Roddick directly
towards Charing Cross. Harding had had to wait some time
for the ground to dry and began his move at two o'clock,
but it was a slow and painful process. Only 20 miles had
been covered by dark, and the wear and tear on the tanks, all
old before the battle started, reduced Roberts' brigade to 47
Grants and Shermans, 15 Stuarts and 30 Crusaders.

Rommel had been given a most welcome breathing space

in which to pull together the remnants of his army. He had
the advantage of having a metalled road behind him, although
lack of petrol and the target presented to the air by his
congested traffic at Sollum and Halfaya offset it to a certain
degree. He had been visited by General Gandin on behalf
of Cavallero, and had shaken the representative of Comando
Supremo by making it perfectly clear that in the swiftest
possible retreat to the maximum distance lay the only hope
of saving the little that still survived of the Panzer Armee,
which only a few months before had seen the Nile Valley at
its feet. No stand to save any part of Cyrenaica or Tripolitania would be possible, and even the retreat would be pre-
judiced by lack of petrol. The picture was black enough, but
it was to be made blacker still next day when the news broke
of the Anglo-American landings at the other end of the
Mediterranean. 'Lightfoot' and 'Supercharge' were over:
'Torch' had now begun.

The battle of El Alamein was a resounding victory, achieved just in time to precede Eisenhower's landings at the other end of the Mediterranean. It came as a real tonic to the British people who celebrated it by ringing church bells, silent for three years, after Churchill had prudently awaited the result of the North African assault. It is difficult to discover any reliable figure for Rommel's losses as far as men killed and wounded is concerned. Of a total strength of probably a little over 100,000 at the beginning of the battle, 30,000, of which 10,000 were German, were taken prisoner, although. the Germans themselves gave a much lower figure (1,100 Germans killed, 3,900 wounded: 1,200 Italians killed, 1,600 wounded). Rommel certainly left about 1,000 guns and 450 of his 600 tanks on the battlefield. The Italians abandoned about 75 tanks during the retreat for lack of fuel. The Afrika Korps cannot have had more than about 20 tanks, if that, left when they withdrew from Mersa Matruh on November 8th: by the time they had reorganised at Mersa Brega a week later, they had collected a total of 80. Of the infantry 90th Light and 164th Division could produce about one regimental group each, but the Italian divisions had virtually disintegrated. That Rommel's next serious stand, on the Mareth Line, was made 1,500 miles further west four months later is an indication of the extent of his defeat.

8th Army's casualties of all kinds had been 13,500, just under eight per cent of the forces engaged; 500 tanks had been put out of action, but only 150 were destroyed beyond repair; and 100 guns had been destroyed either by enemy action or premature shell bursts. This was not a high price to pay for the results achieved. There are those who suggest that the victory could have been even more complete; that it could have been achieved at less cost or even that the battle could have been avoided altogether, the opportunity of defeating Rommel having already been presented at Alam el Halfa.

There are many interesting avenues of speculation which can be explored, the limits being set only by the imagination or the time available. First in time is what the result would have been if Rommel had obeyed his original orders and taken the advice of Westphal in halting at the frontier of Egypt after his capture of Tobruk. If his masters had then decided to concentrate on capturing Malta, the history of the war in the Mediterranean would certainly have been different. If, as is likely, they still shrank from it, it is true that Rommel might have been no better off further west, with an open desert flank and the Desert Air Force nearer Tobruk and Benghazi, than he eventually found himself after Alam el Halfa at El Alamein. Would Ritchie and Auchinleck have remained? Would pressure to relieve Malta not have forced 8th Army to attack again before its superiority was so overwhelming as to make victory certain? The odds on whether it was a good or a bad decision by Rommel are probably even: but there is no doubt that in many ways the enforced withdrawal to El Alamein was a blessing in disguise to 8th Army.

Rommel himself has speculated on the possibility of an alternative to his remaining at El Alamein after Alam el Halfa. The plan, which he never in fact proposed before the battle, would have been to withdraw his immobile troops to a new line at Fuka, while his mobile forces continued to act as a rearguard on the minefields at El Alamein. He himself dismisses it as impracticable in the circumstances of the time and admits that it could not have served as more than a delaying position. He glosses over the difficulties of withdrawing to and constructing the new line, and assumes that Montgomery would have waited until he was installed there before launching his attack.

What course would events have taken if Gott had not been killed? It is probable that it would have made little difference to the result of Alam el Halfa, but it is difficult to imagine Gott facing the prolonged attrition of El Alamein or even planning for it. Like Montgomery he was greatly influenced by his experiences of the First World War, but his reaction took a different form. Montgomery was appalled at the inefficiency and lack of professional skill which led to failures and heavy casualties. It was not so much the casualties themselves which horrified him as the waste, because nothing was achieved by them. He did not shrink from the direct approach, if it were efficiently done. Gott on the other hand was determined to avoid a repetition of anything that even resembled First World War operations. He sought an alternative in the mobile battle and the indirect approach, as Rommel did. His mind was already searching for possible alternatives to a direct assault and considering long-ranging moves through Siwa. The facts of geography were against him, and there is little doubt that Brooke was right in preferring Montgomery for the particular task that inevitably lay ahead of 8th Army.

Was the battle really necessary? Could not Montgomery have delivered the 'coup de grâce' at Alam el Halfa? Theoretically it would seem that he might have done, and it is clear that at first he thought so too. If a swift riposte had been planned on the first day and rapidly executed, it might have succeeded; but the disappointing results of the action of 8th Armoured Brigade on the morning of September 1st and of the New Zealand Division on the night of the 3rd showed him only too clearly how blunt was the weapon in his hand when it came to attack. Montgomery was a realist, and there is no doubt that persistence in counter-attack at that time would have gained him little and led to losses which he would regret later. It is much more difficult to be positive over the controversy concerning his initial attack. There is much to be said for the view, which united Lumsden and Freyberg, that the infantry should have taken a second bite at the cherry to complete their task on the second night, before the attempt was made to push 10th Corps through. In spite of the obvious difficulties of completing all that had to be done in one night, the experience of the battle however goes far to justify Montgomery's decision. Of the infantry divisions which took part in the initial attack, only 9th Australian was in a fit state to undertake any serious operation on the following night, and in their sector that could certainly not have been foreseen. To have had sufficient infantry avail-

able for a second major blow twenty-four hours after the
first would have meant either restricting the front of the
initial attack, already reduced to six miles, or abandoning
any attempt at simulating or executing offensive operations on
the whole of 13th Corps' front. Furthermore the day's
pause between the attacks would have given the enemy even
greater opportunity to see exactly where the blow was falling
and to take measures to seal it off. When one considers that
the whole of Lumsden's armour was held up for several days
on the Rahman track at the very end of the battle by the much
reduced forces then available to Rommel, one must be inclined to think that the armour would have had just as
much, if not more, difficulty in breaking out, if they had
waited until the second morning, than they had on the first.

It has also been suggested that Montgomery could have
broken through more quickly and at less cost if he had not
attacked in the north where the enemy was strongest. The
alternatives were either between Ruweisat and Bare Ridges,
where most of the battles of July had taken place, or between
Munassib and Himeimat. The second had many disadvantages,
the principal being that any attack would tend to be funnelled into the narrow neck of good going just north of Gebel
Kalakh and that Rommel had ready-made positions, covered
by his own old minefields, on which to fall back in that
area. The central sector promised little if any advantage
over the northern. The defences were almost as strong and
well mined. Any penetration here would be less of an immediate threat to Rommel and would make it easier for him
to concentrate his mobile forces to meet it without seriously
endangering other sectors. The violence of the Panzer Armee's
reactions, and particularly Rommel's, to the threat posed
throughout the battle by the salient near Kidney Ridge, is
eloquent proof of the soundness of its choice as the direction
of the main thrust, if a direct assault could not be avoided
and invitation to counter-attack was to be the aim. Whether
the second thrust should have come north of the salient as it
did, or have been a renewal of the original plan to thrust
out from Miteiriya Ridge, is a more difficult question to
answer. One cannot but feel that one more determined push
on the southern flank might have got through and led to the

sequence of events which followed 'Supercharge' a great deal
earlier. But two attempts to get Gatehouse to thrust out there
had already failed. By chance the Australians were in a better
state to launch a determined attack than any other division at
the time. Without any major redeployment of infantry or
artillery they could do so in an area which produced an
immediate and direct threat to Rommel. Although neither
their first nor their second attack led to the intended result
of a break-through on the coast, nor even to the capture of
their own more limited objectives, they had a profounder
effect on the battle than could reasonably have been expected.
Rommel's reaction was immediate and, despite the sound
advice of his subordinates, he persisted in counter-attacks in
that area which brought needless losses and left him much
less capable of dealing with 'Supercharge'. Throughout the
battle Rommel's counter-attacks achieved nothing but casualties to his own forces. Some were hardly noticed by his opponents. Stumme's more cautious policy of containment and
local limited counter-attacks might have cost less; but at
most would only have prolonged the battle by a few days.
The issue could never be in real doubt.

In spite of the effect which the Australian attacks in
the north undoubtedly had, it was fortunate that Montgomery
was dissuaded from proceeding with them and that he decided to switch his efforts back to the original area. 'Supercharge' did not hit the Italians, as expected initially and
claimed afterwards, but struck a portion of the front held
by 15th Panzer Division. The belief that it would avoid the
Germans was based on information that Trieste Division had
taken over that sector of the front. In fact the division was
split, part of it being north of 15th Panzer and part south.
The final break-out did in fact come through its southern
sector. It is possible that it might have been achieved more
easily and quickly if the first blow had been slightly further
south, but the Afrika Korps would itself probably have been
switched further south to meet it, so that the result might not
have been very different, and the going would have included
the soft patches which troubled 5th Indian Brigade later.

One band of critics, including Rommel, accused Montgomery of 'astonishing caution' in restricting attacks to local

limited actions. Others accuse him of reckless expenditure of lives and material by persisting in attacks against the enemy's strongest defences and, in particular, of throwing away his tanks by forcing them to debouch from narrow lanes in the face of enemy defences which were still intact. Certainly his plan was not a cautious one at any time, however cautiously it may have been executed. If he is to be criticised on the grounds of caution, it could be that greater risks might have been taken over freeing forces from holding the front line in order to speed up the redeployment of formations, which was such a critical factor in delaying the start of another fresh attack.

The validity of the criticism of reckless or unnecessary expenditure of lives and tanks depends upon the degree of casualties in a battle of this nature which is to be regarded as reasonable. Is it a human factor or is it solely to be related to the practical consideration of maintaining a potential for future operations? By the standards of previous wars the proportion of casualties to the total force employed was astonishingly low in the light of the results achieved; but figures alone do not tell the whole story. In a modern army, and particularly in the desert where every necessity of life had to be provided and made mobile, the number of men who actually took part in the fighting in sight of the enemy was a very small proportion of the whole. The average infantry battalion would cross the start line with 20 officers and 400 men: a further 130 or thereabouts would join them on the final objective, bringing supporting weapons, wireless and the like. About 250 men of the battalion would take no part in the active fighting. If the 420 of the original attacking force fell to 300, the battalion became incapable of carrying out a further serious attack until reinforcements had been received, absorbed and trained. In armoured regiments the number who went into battle was even smaller. With the full complement of tanks the tank crews of a regiment numbered less than 200. Their fighting strength lay in their Sherman or Grant tanks, of which few regiments went into action with more than 20, and many less. Casualties to tanks and to their crews, which on the whole were light, might appear small in number; but they could nevertheless quickly reduce fighting strength. It was chiefly on this small proportion of fighting men, with their accompanying sappers and anti-tank and other gunners, on whom the great majority of losses fell. There is no doubt that, of the true fighting strength of the divisions engaged, a very high proportion suffered casualties; but that is not to say that they were excessive by whatever standards that is judged, and certainly not so among the armour, either in terms of human casualties or of tanks knocked out. The effect of casualties on morale is not necessarily solely a matter of numbers. The smaller the body of fighting men, the greater the impact on their spirits of the loss of their comrades, particularly if the loss falls, as it did, on the outstanding characters among them.

It it perfectly justifiable to maintain that tank losses could easily have been self-defeating, if the tanks had been made to do what undoubtedly Montgomery at first, and Freyberg all the time, wanted them to do. The question to answer in this respect is whether gallant actions like those of the Royal Wiltshire Yeomanry on October 24th and November 2nd, on both of which occasions they lost almost all their tanks, achieved more or less than the patient but apparently cautious slogging away by Fisher's 2nd Armoured Brigade in the Kidney Ridge salient. To critics the latter appeared to have achieved nothing. However, as we can now see, it achieved a great deal more than the short and gallant actions of 9th Armoured Brigade in terms of casualties to the enemy and particularly to his tanks and anti-tank guns. In fact these actions, fought out in and around the infantry's foremost positions within the range of masses of artillery, achieved exactly what Montgomery intended that the armour should, although he had neither intended nor visualised that they would do so before any break-out had been made. This is not to say that there were not failures. 8th Armoured Brigade could clearly have done more; the maddening muddle early on over where everybody was in the Kidney Ridge area wasted valuable time and effort, and in the latter stages of 'Supercharge' there is little doubt that bolder moves could and should have been made.

In retaliation the armour could justifiably maintain that, at any rate in the case of the Kidney Ridge salient, the infantry in the original attack had not done their job sufficiently to enable the armour to get on with theirs when daylight came, however gallant the efforts to do so might have been.

Although 500 tanks were put out of action during the battle, the fact that only 150 were damaged beyond repair indicates, as appears also from contemporary accounts, that a large number of these were not 'knocked out' by tank or anti-tank gunfire, but only 'disabled' by mines. In such a case the casualties to the crew were normally light, if any, and the damage, broken tracks and smashed suspension, was easily repaired as soon as the tank could be moved from the minefield. Although the anti-tank mine might not do much lasting damage, it was in fact the dominating feature of the battle. In restricting the employment of tanks both in direct support of the infantry and in a more independent and mobile role, it determined both the general and the detailed pattern of the battle. It was the time taken to clear mines which, more than anything else, prevented the tanks from passing through the enemy's defences before it was light. If an efficient mechanical means of mine-clearance had been developed, proved and produced in numbers earlier, the battle would have taken a very different form.

Criticism has been accentuated by the impression given by Montgomery himself that the whole battle went entirely according to plan. He is perfectly justified in maintaining that, in general terms, it did. The night attacks on enemy defences in areas of vital importance to the whole position drew the Panzer Armee, and particularly Rommel when he arrived, to throw in counter-attacks in daylight against the massive fire-power of 8th Army and the Desert Air Force. This wore away their mobile forces while the constant pounding from artillery, combined with the infantry attacks, wore away their static troops, although it appears to have borne little relation to the concept of 'crumbling' in the original plan. It was a battle of attrition rather than movement, but ever since Montgomery had modified his plan early in October, he had intended it to be. It may have been expensive and unromantic, but it made certain of victory, and the certainty of victory at that time was all important. 8th Army had the resources to stand such a battle, while the Panzer Armee had not, and Montgomery had the determination, will-power and ruthlessness to see such a battle through.

Just because the battle did not follow the course mapped for it, the organisation of command soon became inappropriate. If Lumsden's 10th Corps had been right out on its own, well clear of the area captured by Leese's 30th Corps, it would have been perfectly suitable; but, as it was, the superimposition of one corps on another and the duplication, confusion and opportunity for disagreement to which it gave rise, undoubtedly led to inefficiency and missed opportunities. Montgomery cannot escape blame for allowing this to continue beyond the time when it was no longer unavoidable, by leaving the New Zealand Division under Leese's command although it was leading the pursuit after 'Supercharge'.

In fact the handling of the operations of the last few days is clearly open to criticism. The choice of the New Zealand Division to lead the pursuit was a curious one and cannot be explained only on the ground of personal choice; that Freyberg was the only commander at that stage whom Montgomery felt he could trust to be sufficiently thrusting; or on grounds of caution; that he thought that the task of holding the retreating remnants of the Panzer Armee was one which required more infantry than an armoured division could provide. It is now clear that the sudden arrival of torrential rain on November 6th was in no way responsible for the failure to cut off more of the remnants of the Panzer Armee. Even if 1st Armoured Division had started off on its long left hook from Daba to Charing Cross sooner after it had been told to and had not suffered from its failures of petrol supply, Briggs could not have reached Charing Cross before Rommel, although his arrival in that area might have hastened the latter's departure from Mersa Matruh. More significant and frustrating was the maddening delay on November 5th over the minefield south of Fuka, which in the end proved to be a British-laid dummy; but even in that case neither Freyberg nor Harding could have got much further that evening for lack of petrol. With all the advantages of hindsight it is now clear that the real opportunity arose and was missed in the early hours of November 5th.

The air report during the night made it clear that Rommel was off, and that the movement of 1st and 7th Armoured Divisions towards Daba would miss him. It was also known, long before it was light, that neither Freyberg nor Custance had moved as was planned, and that their chances of cutting off any considerable number of the enemy were small also. In spite of this, practically no alteration to the previous orders was made. Little value was then to be gained from sending even one armoured division to Daba. To send two was indeed a work of supererogation. The original orders, which had been that neither division should move at all that morning, were sounder than the decision to send one, and certainly better than the decision to send both to Daba. Montgomery had in 7th Armoured Division a formation comparatively fresh, even if its tanks were not in their first youth, extremely experienced in the problems of long desert moves, and with commanders in Harding and Roberts about whose spirit and skill he could have no doubts. They were well placed, and Roddick's 4th Light Armoured Brigade, which really belonged to Harding too, was ideally situated to switch to his command and take the lead. If, in the early hours of November 5th, Harding had been told to go straight for Charing Cross with Roddick and Roberts, there is little doubt that he might have beaten Rommel to it. Caution may have played a part; the insistence of Coningham on the need to open new landing grounds further forward as soon as possible, and the demands of his logisticians to open up the coast road, may have influenced Montgomery more than they should have done. Bolder action by all concerned on the previous day would have helped a great deal: in any case it is by no means certain that the force which could have reached Charing Cross would have achieved much more than in fact Harding did at Qasaba on the 6th. The man who wants to get away in the desert, and has the vehicles to do so, can usually evade his pursuer, certainly if he is as determined and swift in action and decision as Rommel was.

That Montgomery on the one side and Rommel on the other were the decisive figures is never at any time in doubt. They decided every move; but their own power evaporated when it came to the execution of their decisions in the front line. There decision lay at the level of the battalion or the company commander. He could and did decide whether to struggle on and, if so, how: to stop or, occasionally, to go back. His superiors at brigade, division or corps, who had made the plan, allotted the objectives, arranged the support of tanks, artillery and engineers, and fixed the time, no longer had any say and, in the case of infantry attacks, little power to control events. They were lucky if they even knew what had happened until several hours later, and then only in the broadest terms. Between the army commander and the commanding officer, brigadiers and generals could interpose in planning and could distort or delay in execution; but their power and freedom of action was at all times severely limited. Freyberg could flit to and fro behind the scenes, but the real effect of his intervention was less than appeared. Such power as these intermediate figures wielded was generally more easily exercised negatively than positively as in the case of the caution imposed by Lumsden, Gatehouse, Custance and others. The combined pressure of men of such energy, spirit and resource as Horrocks, Harding and Roberts could avail little against the hard facts of reality down by Himeimat.

To the infantryman in the attack or sitting it out day after day in his slit trench in the front line; to the tank crew, grinding forward in the dark and dust among the mines or trying to edge forward by day towards the ridge from which the anti-tank guns were firing; to the sappers clearing the mines, the anti-tank gunners and, to a lesser extent, the other gunners, it frequently seemed a chaotic and ghastly muddle. The area of the salient east of Kidney Ridge was the worst of all. The whole place was knee deep in dust. Nobody knew where anybody or anything was, where minefields started or ended. There was always somebody firing at something and usually somebody being fired at, but who and what it was and why was generally a mystery. To try and find out led from one false clue to another. The information one gleaned would probably be wrong anyway. In the end one gave up trying to 'tie everything up' and went one's own sweet way, hardening one's heart to the inconvenience, annoyance or anger it might cause to somebody else. The longer the battle went on, the less patient one became, the less inclined to obey orders and generally take trouble. The sudden glimpse of daylight, as the front began to break in the first few days of November, blew all this weariness of spirit away. Now it was a race for who should be first out, tempered by the feeling that, having miraculously survived the ever-present dangers of the battle among the minefields, it would be folly to fling away one's life too recklessly when victory was at hand.

In the exhilaration of victory after so many disappointments there was little time for sympathy for one's enemy. Twenty years later, looking back without bitterness, one cannot but sympathise with the Panzer Armee, who fought so gallantly against hopeless odds, and particularly with its commander, Erwin Rommel. He saw the army, which he had created from practically nothing and led with such distinction almost to its goal, shattered before his eyes, all hope of rebuilding it removed by the news that the Allies had landed at the far end of the Mediterranean.

Rommel lays the blame for most of his losses in the final stages of the battle, particularly for the abandonment of his immobile Italian infantry, on the order from Hitler, received on the afternoon of November 3rd, countermanding the order for withdrawal which he had given the night before. In fact it is difficult to see that it made much difference, as the attempt to put it into effect does not appear to have succeeded, even if it were really seriously made. With the possible exception of Bologna in the central sector, who were unlikely to have been able to escape westwards in any case, it appears that both in the north and the south the Panzer Armee did in fact continue to withdraw in the 24 hours during which the countermanding order remained in force.

For Montgomery himself and for his 8th Army it was indeed a great victory. Of it Churchill wrote that it could almost be said: 'Before Alamein we never had a victory. After Alamein we never had a defeat.' 'Almost' is a necessary qualification, considering the earlier victories in the desert and in Abyssinia. Together with the failure of the Germans to capture Stalingrad at the same time, it marked the turning point of the Second

World War. The victory was won by the determination, realism and professional skill of Montgomery; the greatly superior material at his disposal, particularly in terms of fire-power delivered by gun, tank and aircraft; his superiority in numbers of men, and the courage and dogged persistence in the firing line of a comparatively small number of soldiers, chiefly infantry, tank crews, sappers and anti-tank gunners. The contribution of others, soldiers, airmen and sailors, was essential; but it was upon this smaller body of men that the burden of battle and its inevitable casualties fell. Many of them still lie beneath the sand at El Alamein. As in all battles the dead and the wounded came chiefly from the bravest and the best.

CHRONOLOGY OF THE BATTLE 1942

August

3rd   Churchill and Brooke arrive in Cairo.

5th   They visit 8th Army.

6th   Alexander chosen for Middle East and Gott for 8th Army.

7th   Gott killed. Montgomery chosen to replace him.

9th   Alexander reaches Cairo.

12th   Montgomery reaches Cairo: sees Auchinleck.

13th   Montgomery visits 8th Army and prematurely assumes command.

15th   Alexander takes over from Auchinleck.

19th   Churchill and Brooke visit 8th Army.

30th   (*night*) Rommel attacks. Start of Battle of Alam el Halfa.

31st   Action round Alam el Halfa.

September

1st   8th Armoured Brigade action. Heavy RAF attacks.

2nd   Rommel decides to withdraw.

3rd   New Zealand Division attack fails.

5th   Rommel's final withdrawal. Battle ends.

19th   Stumme arrives to relieve Rommel.

23rd   Rommel departs on sick leave.

October

23rd   (*night*) Battle of El Alamein opens.

24th   All divisions of 8th Army on general line of Axis main defences. Stumme dies in action.
      (*night*) Abortive attempt by 10th Armoured Division to break out through New Zealand Division, and by 7th Armoured Division to break through minefields near Himeimat.

25th   Montgomery abandons attempt to get both 10th and 7th Armoured Divisions out: orders 9th Australian

Division to start 'crumbling' in North and 1st Armoured Division to 'operate West' in Kidney Ridge
area. Rommel returns.

(*night*) Australian attack partially successful. No progress by 1st Armoured Division.

26th   Repeated Axis attacks in Kidney Ridge area make no
impact and suffer severe casualties. Montgomery
reconsiders: orders 10th Corps to 'make progress' and
Australians to attack on 28th.

(*night*) 1st Armoured Division attacks in Kidney
Ridge area.

27th   Rifle Brigade action at *Snipe*. No advance by tanks of
1st Armoured Division. Repeated Axis attacks suffer
heavy casualties.

28th   Montgomery abandons thrust in Kidney Ridge area.
Main effort to be in North, exploiting Australian attack. Rommel moves up all German units from South.
(*night*) Very limited success of Australian attack.
Rommel decides to make one more attempt to stand;
but if pressure too great to withdraw to Fuka.

29th   Doubts at home. Visit of Alexander and Casey. Montgomery finally decides to abandon coastal thrust and
plans *Supercharge,* a fresh effort north of Kidney
Ridge. New Zealand Division to attack on night of
31st, followed by 10th Corps.

30th   (*night*) Renewed Australian attack in Thompson's
Post area establishes depleted 26 Brigade on coast
road. Freyberg requests postponement of *Supercharge.*

31st   *Supercharge* postponed to night November 1st/2nd.
German attacks on 26 Australian Brigade fail. Relieved
by 24 Brigade. 7th Armoured Division move up from
South.

November

1st   Repeated attacks on 24 Australian Brigade finally force
them south of railway, and pocket of Germans escape.

2nd   *Supercharge* starts: reaches Rahman track. Confusion
in Afrika Korps. Fierce and repeated Axis attacks.
Montgomery plans break-out south of Kidney Ridge,

where Axis weakness revealed and Royals armoured cars got through.

Rommel decides to withdraw and informs Hitler.

3rd   10 Corps attempt to break out fails. Lull in battle. Axis withdrawal starts: countermanded by Hitler.

     (*night*) Slight general withdrawal by Afrika Korps.

4th   1st Armoured Division and Afrika Korps battle round Tel el Aqqaqir. 7th Armoured and New Zealand Divisions break out further south. Rommel outflanked orders general withdrawal to Fuka.

     (*night*) No forward move by 8th Army, although ordered.

5th   Start of pursuit. 8th Armoured Brigade catch remnants of XX Corps near Galal. New Zealand and 7th Armoured Divisions held up by dummy minefield and lack of petrol south of Fuka. 1st Armoured Division ordered to Bir Khalda and 'Charing Cross': slow start and move. Rommel withdraws from Fuka.

6th   1st Armoured Division held up by lack of petrol. 7th Armoured Division engages 21st Panzer Division, which is out of petrol. Rain falls.

7th   10th Armoured Division ordered along coast road to Mersa Matruh. Slow progress and held up on arrival.

     (*night*) Rommel withdraws to Sollum.

8th   Operation *Torch*. Allied landings in North Africa under Eisenhower.

INDEX